THE WOLSELEY SHOWROOMS IN
PICCADILLY, LONDON, W.

BREAKFAST
at
The WOLSELEY

A. A. GILL

Photography by David Loftus

Hardie Grant

QUADRILLE

CONTENTS

160 PICCADILLY

It often comes as a surprise to a visitor walking through the doors of The Wolseley to discover that this seemingly *fin de siècle* restaurant only opened in the early twenty-first century. Although originally built in the 1920s, it wasn't until 2003 that Chris Corbin and Jeremy King saw its potential to be the *grand café* in the European tradition that Londoners only found on the Continent, and for which they much envied Paris, Munich, Vienna, Budapest, *et al*. It perhaps comes as a greater shock to learn that this unique building, the first significant work of architect William Curtis Green, who subsequently built The Dorchester, was originally commissioned as a showroom for cars.

The grandness of the building owed its scale to the ambitions of The Wolseley Car Company and its desire to capitalize on the vast expansion in public knowledge of, and interest in, motoring in Britain post 1918, in the era following the Great War. The company was founded by Frederick York Wolseley, an Irishman who emigrated to Australia in the 1850s to become a sheep farmer and, subsequently, to form the hugely successful Wolseley Sheep Shearing Company. The development of this company's innovative machines provided the engineering and technical expertise that led to Wolseley's successor, Herbert Austin, producing the first Wolseley car in 1896, after the company had transferred its operations back to London. The early Wolseley cars, pioneers in the history of British motoring, commenced full production in 1901. With the increased manufacturing capacity no longer required for the

production of wartime aeroplane engines, the company could capitalize on the public's demand for new cars. In 1920 it commissioned Curtis Green to build a West End showroom next to The Ritz hotel, introducing the fashion for luxury car showrooms in Mayfair and St James's. By the time Wolseley House was completed by Cubitts in 1921, at a cost of £250,000, the company was achieving significant speed records at Brooklands and was confident of expanding markets.

Wolseley House, watercolour submitted to the Royal Academy by W. Curtis Green, *1919*

Until this commission, Curtis Green had been largely restricted to comparatively mundane house-building in the great suburban spread. This might explain his apparent desire to draw upon so many architectural influences. The main inspiration came from Brunelleschi's Santo Spirito in Florence, with the geometric marble floors modelled on those of churches from Pisa and San Marco in Venice. However, the Italianate influences were joined by many others: Byzantine light fittings, baroque ironwork, Doric interior and Corinthian exterior columns, all finished off with Wren-like touches and even a mansard roof in the French style. All this was juxtaposed with elaborate japan-lacquered screens and decorations that exemplified fashionable Mayfair's taste in the 1920s for Eastern exoticism. It was noted at the time that 'This building seems a counterpoint to the philosophy that less is more', and indeed it sits in striking contrast to the more understated and orthodox treatment of Curtis Green's 1927 National Westminster Bank across the road at 63 Piccadilly.

In 1923, Curtis Green received the Royal Institute of British Architects' Street Architecture Medal and was moved to give thanks 'that Wolseley Motors had the foresight, unusual in this country, to see that architecture is a commercial asset'.

Sadly, Wolseley cars failed to sell in the anticipated numbers and, on the verge of bankruptcy, the company sold the building in 1926 to Barclays Bank. Barclays invited Curtis Green to return and carry out the conversion

The wedding procession of Her Royal Highness Princess Mary of York passing Wolseley House, *28 February 1922*

to a banking hall. He added managers' offices either side of the main door (now serving as a bar and tea salon), but instead of retreating into the safe, traditional banking décor of green leather and mahogany panelling, he further developed the Eastern theme. Even more gold and black japan lacquer was employed: the treatment extended to furniture and fittings, including the banking counter and postbox which are on view to this day.

Barclays Bank enjoyed its reputation as the most elegant and exotic of banking halls until it, too, bowed to the pressures of decentralization and left in 1998. When Corbin and King acquired the lease, they asked architect David Collins to complete its transition into The Wolseley Café and Restaurant. His sensitive treatment of the interior has engendered the sense of timelessness that has enabled The Wolseley to rapidly gain its iconic status for Londoners and visitors alike.

Artist's impression of the interior, *c. 1921*

Breakfast is everything. The beginning, the first thing. It is the mouthful that is the commitment to a new day, a continuing life. As meals change with the ages, climate and geography, move round the clock, disappear into the night, come back shrunk or instant, breakfast remains a constant, a fixed point all around the world. It is one of the very few things that link every one of us to everyone else.

Breakfast — simple, elaborate, hurried, deliberate or skipped — is an unconsidered moment of global communion. Somewhere, someone is starting breakfast and thinking, 'Today will be better than yesterday.' Someone is gulping coffee before opening the bills, is dropping marmalade onto the paper, is shouting up the stairs, is hunting for homework or a briefcase, is listening to the still, long dawn shadows in the chilly desert, is watching the mist clear from the canopy of the rainforest, is ignoring the commuters' roar from a packing-case house under a motorway flyover, is blearily trying to rub life into a numb leg as the stewardess asks if he or she would like the healthy option in the thin, dark air above us. Wherever, whenever breakfast comes, it's a mouthful of stoic optimism.

Breakfast is a meal apart. It isn't like the other organized consumptions of food in which we all take part. Even though it's a fixed moment, breakfast is pre-form — a conceptual meal. It doesn't have courses or an order; it isn't prescriptively sweet or savoury; there is no generally accepted sense of its length or constituent parts. It's bespoke, tailor-made to you: a private meal or habit. Breakfast is the most personal and idiosyncratic construction. It is the only meal most of us feel wholly comfortable eating on our own; it's the one meal we feel most uncomfortable having to share with strangers. It is the most intimate of meals, a euphemism, a glance and a sly smile.

One of the things that distinguishes us as a species is our inquisitive desire for change, novelty and experimentation. Every other living organism looks for a dependable, plentiful and sustained food source and then sticks

with it. Your dog, for example, may eat the same tin of pooch slop every day of its life with an identical ravenous joy. He may also eat any human leftovers – but not with the spirit of gastronomic enquiry or epicurean pleasure. He may not necessarily distinguish between cheese and chocolate; it's all just food. Yet humans will go to great lengths to discover something different to eat: climbing hundreds of feet into pitch-black caves for congealed swallow spit; risking death by a thousand stings to smoke wild

beehives for honey; sailing into the utterly unknown on a ship that's smaller than a semi-detached cottage on a promise of nutmeg and cloves. The yearning for variety, the active horror of sameness, has been one of the governing engines of civilization. We won't eat the same thing two meals in a row – except for breakfast.

Breakfast is the only exception, the only meal where we expect the comfort and confirmation of predictability, where we become like dogs. We want the same bowl of cereal, the same piece of toast, the same cup of tea all our adult lives. Indeed, choosing your life's breakfast is one of the small decisions that mark you as a grown-up: setting aside the sugar-crusted, multicoloured, zoomorphically shaped processed carbs of childhood for the sombre, brown, bran-rich, blandly goodly flakes of colonic probity and adulthood. Breakfast may be the closest we ever get to communing with our pre-agricultural hunter-gathering ancestors. It may well be the meal in which, despite microwave porridge, instant cappuccino, hydrogenated breakfast bars and low-fat smoothies, the manner and imperative of eating has remained constant throughout our collective history. Unconsidered, unreported and unmemorable, the habits of breakfasts have been passed down the ages, hand to mouth.

Piccadilly is chilly and dark. There's precious little traffic: occasional questing taxis; late-night salesmen a long way from home; minicab drivers from the rough and dangerous edges of the world plying a precarious living, kept up by khat and amphetamines and the thought of their less-lucky families across the globe; and those mysterious cyclists bent in half, heads down, pedalling for their lives.

Through the windows of The Wolseley seeps a pale yellow light. The building is Alderman and imposing, built to impress. Originally it was a car showroom for Wolseleys, then it became a bank. Now it's a restaurant that serves all the meals a well-ordered life could demand: lunch, tea, dinner and, of course, breakfast. No sooner have the waiters handed the coats and smiled at the last of the dinner customers, who look at their watches and say, 'God, I'd no idea it was that late!' than the room has to get going again for its next meal. In the basement, the kitchen never grows cold: the blue-tongued hobs and crisping ovens, the hissing salamanders relax for a moment in their reflected warmth. The monumental bronze street doors are shut for an hour or two's respite, but in the dining room the cleaners are working.

A jolly Nigerian wears bright-blue industrial rubber gloves and, in a giant fist, holds aloft a Day-Glo feather duster like a sceptre or a dictator's fly-whisk. As a tool of a trade it is undeservedly comic. Cleaning is hard, thankless, boring drudgery: there's precious little that's funny about it, and you have to carry your own sense of amusement and achievement like a packed lunch. He has been working here for three months. He lives in South London; when he's finished this shift, he'll go to college, where he's studying social work. And when he's done that, some homework and had something to eat, he'll get an eyeful of sleep. He laughs: the big, rumbling, resigned laugh of a hard African life. Yes, it's tough, but it's better. He fences with the dust on the many flat surfaces, like a conductor directing a comic opera. His three mates circle the room with mop and bucket and the box of polishes, disinfectants, cloths and sponges that is the make-up box of a well-groomed dining room.

VIENNOISERIE

The first person to go back into the kitchen is the *tourier*. His is an archaic calling; there are very few *touriers* left in professional kitchens. He is the risen-pastry maker. *Tourier* comes from the word 'turning', as in turning dough. He's not strictly a baker, or a *pâtissier*, or a confectioner; he is a *tourier*. When Carème, the man more responsible than any for inventing the stations of a modern commercial kitchen, named the jobs of cuisine, he ordained that there should be a *tourier*, and so here, at The Wolseley, there is. He is a man, if not obsessed, then utterly absorbed by his trade, his craft.

First thing are the croissants, the most internationally well-travelled and defining breakfast breads. You can be pretty sure of getting a croissant in every international hotel and metropolitan café with cosmopolitan pretensions in the world. I have been offered croissants from Ho Chi Minh City to N'Djamena. It is a sophisticated pastry that has been transformed by endless repetition into a flabby, fast-food comestible. Few things have been so roundly, squarely and obliquely abused as the croissant: stuffed with scrambled egg and bacon, Swiss cheese and epidermal ham, soft and tasteless, its butter replaced with vegetable oil. The croissant is a malformed, uncared-for victim of international convenience, and whenever you find a real one it can come as a surprise. This is not the boomerang-shaped, soggy bun you remember from your economy inflight breakfast tray, but an architecturally daring edifice of cantilevered layers that seem to be held up by impossible physics. A skin of brittle delicacy, like sun-tanned eggshell, and an inside that is surprisingly robust and chewy…it is that combination that is its particular allure. It's the butter that does it: the folded layers of butter-infused, enthused pastry, the heat of the oven expanding the air, lifting it, puffing it up to set in its perfect, undulating, spherical shape. The *tourier* leans over his dough, folding and shaping with a practised economy. Watching craftsmen craft is one of the quietest and deepest pleasures of a cack-handed life. The *tourier* arranges the pastry-pale, embryonic croissants on a slick baking tray and slides them into a rainforest-hot oven.

Part of the croissant's attraction has always been its Parisian *savoir faire* – it's always assumed that they are French. In England and America, the croissant is the central ingredient in the ubiquitous Continental breakfast, the cellophane-wrapped give-away of budget hotels, the Continental appellation offered as a sop of *je ne sais quoi*, a consolation for its grim frugality. The inclusive, free Continental breakfast may well be the least hospitable act in the whole of catering. 'Continental', to excuse its appetite-quenching nastiness, is like mentioning that an ugly, foul-tempered girl has a father who owns a pub – it's the association that adds lustre. The Continent, for the English and Americans, starts with Paris. The croissant comes with all the can-can of pastry. The truth is, it isn't French at all.

Tracing the origins of dishes and ingredients is notoriously prone to mythologizing. There are cogent commercial and patriotic reasons for attaching ownership and romance to a dish, but as far as we can tell, the croissant is about as French as the waltz. It's Austrian. It comes as part of what the French call collectively *Viennoiserie* – pastries from Vienna. The first croissant was made in 1683, a date that should be the most famous in Europe, not because of breakfast, but because of the breaking of the siege of Vienna. After 300 years of incessant conflict, this marked the beginning of the end of the Turkish-Muslim expansion west. Vienna was the make-or-break city on the Danube: it would have opened central Europe to Turkish rule, and they very nearly made it.

Victory at the gates of Vienna was confirmation that the age of European world domination had begun; a moment in history where a door opened and a door closed. It is also said, retrospectively, to be the first pan-European confederation, the collective effort on behalf of the Continent, and is still seen in strictly religious terms (Christian versus Muslim), although it was not that simple. The Catholic French used the siege as an excuse to plunder southern Germany, annex Strasbourg and claim Alsace. And the Turks' greatest allies were Protestant Christian Hungarians who were revolting against the expansion of the rapidly counter-reforming Habsburgs in Vienna. It's a forgotten but toothsome irony that it was the sort of Protestants who today are the most fiercely anti-Islamic who fought with the Muslims to defeat a Catholic Europe. Anyway, it's breakfast, and there are more important things afoot. A baker in Vienna invented the croissant in the shape of the Sultan symbol of Islam to commemorate the victory. The French believe it was brought to Paris by Marie-Antoinette, an Austrian princess. It might well have been the 'cake' she suggested they ate if they couldn't get bread – so they got rid of her, but kept her breakfast.

The siege of Vienna may well have done more for breakfast than any other historical event. The fleeing Turks left behind their baggage, in which were quantities of coffee; an enterprising Viennese, Francieszek Jerzy Kulczycki, opened Europe's third coffee shop, although I don't expect he named it after himself. The first is always said to be Café Florian, in St Mark's Square, Venice, where you can still get a cup of coffee in a beautiful room that won't have a single Italian in it who isn't wearing

an apron. Viennese cafés served a variation of Arab coffee until, legend has it, a monk, Marco d'Aviano, advisor to the Holy Roman Emperor, added milk and honey to cut the bitterness of his. The drink imitated the white cowl of his robe – he was a Capuchin monk – and so was christened the cappuccino, which got to Italy with the later Austrian occupation.

There we have the Euro ying and yang of breakfast: one half from France, the other from Italy, both in fact from Vienna by way of Istanbul and Ulan Bator. Cappuccino and croissant are the taste of our political, social and geographic union, and Christian civilization: every morning a small taste of history, a covenant with our continent and our culture.

Italians have an odd relationship with cappuccinos; they are by nature a nationality that is pickier than Siamese cats with colic. Italians are the most conservative eaters on the globe – they really don't like anyone else's food. In fact, they'll only eat the dinner of the town next door if there's nothing else. They're also superstitious hypochondriacs, and they're particularly weird about milk, which they think is so difficult to digest as to be almost poisonous. So cappuccino should never, ever, be drunk after 11 o'clock in the morning to give your body time to deal with the intractable bovine gut truculence. And never, EVER order one at the end of a meal. You might as well go out and suck a hospice door handle.

Coffee and croissants aren't the end of the breakfast bounty that springs from the victory of Vienna. It is also said that the bagel was invented to commemorate Jan Sobieski, the Polish king whose intervention saved the city. In particular it's made in the shape of a stirrup to honour the heavy Polish cavalrymen who broke the Turkish line. Bagels are obviously associated with Jewishness – the defining symbol of Ashkenazi Jews. Expecting them to swallow the invention of bagels by Roman Catholic

Austrians is two sandwiches short of a fact: they have their own conception myths for bagels. In one of the many vicious, petty and random pieces of anti-Semitism inflicted on the Diaspora, they were forbidden from baking their bread, so they boiled it – and that's how the bagel was invented. The name comes from the Old German for 'ring'.

And if all that weren't enough largesse, from the fire sale that the siege of Vienna turned out to be, the West also got the instruments that were dropped by retreating Turkish bandsmen. Some say we got the whole idea of military bands from the Turks, but in particular, they gave us (or rather left us) the cymbal, the triangle and the bass drum. What did the Turks get out of the siege of Vienna? A century-long belief that they were more European than Asian, and the fact that the Turkish breakfast is also interesting. In Istanbul they eat *simit*: sesame-covered bread rings not unlike pretzels that hawkers sell on the street. They're eaten with fresh ewes cheese. The Turks gleaned their eclectic cuisine from all over their rolling empire that started with the disgusting food at the central Asian steppe: mares milk and lamb *plov*. It travelled west and folded in Armenian, Greek, Levantine and North African dishes. If you ever eat anything you really like in a Greek restaurant, it's almost certainly Turkish.

Back to the *tourier*, in the early predawn at The Wolseley. It was a long struggle before he managed to master the making of a bagel; other people normally make them better. He has never managed to make a wholly satisfactory crumpet, either, but then I've never heard of anyone who could make a crumpet in a real kitchen.

According to the *Oxford English Dictionary*, the first mention of crumpet is a recipe from 1382, but it doesn't really seem to have appeared in its present sense until the seventeenth century. Alan Davidson marks the earliest recipe as 1769 – actually, it reads as if it would make a thicker drop scone, or pikelet. The word 'crumpet' probably comes from *crempog*, the Welsh for pancake. Elizabeth David, in her exhaustive book on English bread and yeast cooking, notes the collusion between muffin and crumpet: they always seem to travel together. (That is, *English* muffins, not the American cake called a muffin.) Both are made with batter, both are cooked twice and both are served hot with melted butter, but are quite different. She notes tartly, 'Most people have decided preferences for one or the other.' An epicurean friend of considerable appetite always had his crumpets buttered twice, which improves them no end.

But back (again) to the *tourier*. He doesn't make crumpets, but he does make muffins of the American breakfast variety. It's odd how the recipe is so different from ours, and how the sweet cake itself has skipped back two meals from our tea to their breakfast. But then the Americans have done what all children have dreamt of doing for centuries: they've taken teatime and added it to breakfast. They get all the eggy, hammy, porridgy stuff, but with pancakes and doughnuts and teacakes and sweet stuff. You need to discover a new world to be able to make a mould-breaking, etiquette-denying, mummy-defying decision like that.

Having finished the croissants, the *tourier* turns to the *pain au chocolat*. He slips sticks of thick chocolate ganache into the dough. His little neon-lit room begins to smell of warm baking, caramel and chocolate, nutmeg and cinnamon. His assistant, a French *tourier* who's come here from Lyons to learn the intricacies of breakfast pastry, measures chocolate chips for today's muffin. There is a new flavour each morning, just as there is a Danish pastry.

The pastry is filled with a light compote of rhubarb: forced champagne rhubarb grown in dark brick houses in a square mile of south Yorkshire, encouraged to sprout early by candlelight. It has a distinctive pale yellow and pink colour. A century ago, the arrival of the new rhubarb in Covent Garden was as memorable

as the start of the grouse season or the first oysters or asparagus from East Anglia. Rhubarb was the first fresh, sweet, growing thing the Victorians had eaten since the late autumn apples and the last of the greenhouse grapes. They had nearly three months of dried and bottled, sugared, preserved fruits for the ache in their sweet tooth. This rhubarb is about as far from school rhubarb and custard as diamonds are from rhinestones. The compote glistens like varnished coral.

At about 6.30 in the morning the *tourier* will collect all the offerings of his craft and take them up to the restaurant, where he is responsible for arranging the display of breakfast baking: the first thing customers will see as they enter. He carefully makes a pyramid of the croissants; each time he places the last one on the top, they collapse. With a concentrated patience, he builds them up again and stands back for a moment's satisfaction. The Danish pastries, the muffins, the *pain au chocolat,* the sweetened, refined and fortified doughs that have made their way here from across Europe for our breakfast look immaculate.

'We won't sell that many of them,' he says, as a sort of afterthought.

'You can't be serious.'

'Oh, we'll sell some, but a lot will come back down to the staff canteen.'

'That's awful,' I commiserate. 'Don't you mind doing all the work?'

He smiles.

'Oh no, I love making them well, learning new things. They look nice here don't they?'

They look delicious.

'It's not such an English thing to eat pastry for breakfast, you know. Women worry about putting on weight, men about cholesterol and crumbs in their laps.'

This display of *Viennoiserie* is what the owners of The Wolseley call an attitude dish. Not because it's necessarily going to sell terribly well or be popular, but because the sight of it, the knowledge that it's here, tells you something about the dining room, about the restaurant, about what this place thinks of itself, and what it would like you to think of it. It is a statement of intent. A place of assumptions.

'Look, if you're really interested, let me show you something,' says the *tourier*, and takes me into the bar.

The two barmen are beginning to prep their bottles, getting the juices on ice. Today's featured juice is watermelon. On the bar is a plate of fluted cakes the size of a double-or-quits bet of casino chips. They sit beside the wire stand of hard-boiled eggs (there are always eggs on the bar: a hard-boiled attitude).

'Try one of these,' he says, picking up a cake. They have a matt-tan coating, like they've been polished. Inside is an enriched dough. The flavour is delicate and fugitive – a hint of something sweet and complex – the texture like soft, blonde cashmere.

'That's *cannelé de Bordeaux*. I found them on holiday. It's a very old recipe, traditionally from the Bordelais. We use a copper dariole mould and you coat the inside with beeswax, pour in the cake mix and then bake them, and they come out that colour with that lovely finish. The flavour is faintly honeyed.' And so it is.

'I found a guy – a brilliant chap, really – in south London, who's the honey king. He sells organic honeycomb: no additives. So I asked if I could make these. We used to give them away free in the bar, but customers were suspicous so now they're on the menu and they love them. Help yourself.'

A divine, rare, carefully sourced and made, softly spoken, quietly historic mouthful of craftsman's attitude.

In the restaurant the waiters are moving the hundreds and hundreds of individual pieces that have to come together to make a dining room work. People who know restaurants only as customers imagine that they're like theatres. They're actually much more like heavy industry. You're not a player on a stage; you're packaging. The plates of food aren't the product of a restaurant; the customers are. They come in empty and go out full. Working here is rather like being an engineer on a complex shop floor, overseeing a production line that makes an infinite variety of bespoke items simultaneously – and you have to build the factory every morning.

The Wolseley serves four different meals. Each has its own equipment, its condiments, specialist spoons and forks, plates, bowls, doilies, napkins and serving suggestions. Breakfast is a peculiarly complicated meal for waiters because everyone makes up his or her own preferred menu: with this, without that, hold the other, and extra whatnots. We're very finicky about our breakfasts, so the waiters hustle through the dozens of permutations to starting a day.

At the front desk, the *maître d'hôtel* is going through his reservation list, printed off the computer. The phone lines at The Wolseley are answered in another office. Reservations are tapped into a screen where they're all cross-referenced with previous meals. The names come with a code, abbreviations to note 'regular' or 'very regular': the customers who come every week, one or two every day. There are notes on dietary preferences, who they dine with, birthdays, profession. This database is a bit like a benign Stazi report; it contains anything that might help make the service smoother, more personal, that little note that makes a customer preen. Being noticed, being known in a public dining room is one of the smallest but most intense pleasures of a metropolitan life, and these details shape the attitude at The Wolseley.

Today they're full. They're pretty much full every day: 350 confirmed. There will be, perhaps, ten percent who cancel or don't show, then thirty percent who'll walk in on the off-chance. They don't plan to turn the tables here, but most will be used two, three times or more between seven and eleven.

Behind the desk, along with the clipboards, menus, post-its and lost hairgrips, there are also bespoke matches in a complex original Wolseley box. There are Wolseley pads and pencils for customers who are struck by the muse, and behind the *maître d'hôtel* is a machine that will slip a long plastic condom over a wet umbrella. Rain can make the floor treacherous, so there will also be a human hovering with a mop and a cloth. Beside the umbrella-condom machine, there's the paper rack. Every day The Wolseley gets three *Guardians*, three *Daily Telegraphs*, three *Times*, three *Independents*, six *Financial Times*, one *Daily Mirror*, two *Herald Tribunes*, one *El País*, one *Le Monde*, one *Corriere della Sera*, one *Frankfurter Allgemeine*. They're all stamped with The Wolseley's newspaper sticker. You can steal them, but everyone in the office will know you've done it. Later in the day, *Evening Standards* will be added. There is but the one token tabloid. It isn't strictly censorship, just a belief that you should treat customers like guests in your own home.

The international papers are a symbol of the truth of London now: it is Europe's most cosmopolitan city. A dozen nationalities will breakfast here today, and just as many will serve them. On the breakfast shift there is one Italian, one Hungarian, one Filipino, one American, one Brazilian, five Australians, five French, two Syrians, one Israeli, one South African, one Indian, one Egyptian, three Nigerians, one Malian, one Canadian, two Thais, one Swede, one German, one Kiwi, two Slovakians, one Czech, nine Poles, one Zimbabwean and eleven Brits. That's twenty-five countries it takes to serve one breakfast. Between them, they will eat by choice and tradition almost everything grown or husbanded, fished or collected or manufactured at breakfast, and here they are serving what for many of them will be an incongruously bizarre collection of ingredients.

There are few things that are quite as xenophobic as breakfast. If you play the game of 'Whose national cuisine could you live on for the rest of your life?', there are quite a few you could probably manage – until you get to breakfast. Then they shrink to precious few. No one has worked out how many countries the ingredients of The Wolseley's menu come from, or how many nations inspired or originated the combinations. This is a properly international dining room: international in terms of its staff, its clients, its menu, its ingredients, its outlook and its history. The Wolseley is in concept and spirit the descendant of that first Viennese café that invented the cappuccino that went on to be the central stage of grand cafés for that moment when Vienna was the world's most cosmopolitan, open city and the forcing house of great displays of art, science and politics, all of them germinated in cafés.

It isn't that The Wolseley is a pastiche; it's an evolution. On the face of it, it couldn't look more English, more Piccadilly-ish in a Japanese-ish sort of way. Right at the back, on the way to the loo, you'll notice there's a chess set – it's another touch of attitude. It's rather a good chess set, a weighted Stanton set with a knight's head copied from the horse-drawn Phoebus's chariot in the Elgin Marbles. This, of course, being England, few actually play with it, but it's a sign, a symbol. You could if you wanted, and there would be people here who would play with you – probably the staff. Chess is an international game played by Europeans, invented by Arabs, brought to Britain by Vikings.

It's 6.45 a.m., fifteen minutes before the doors open, and the floor manager calls the dining-room staff together for a pep talk. This happens every morning. First of all, she congratulates the staff on the way they handled the crisis yesterday – the Remanco broke. The Remanco is the central nervous system of all restaurants. It is also their great weakness: the chattering copy machine that prints out the orders from the restaurant into the kitchen. If it fails, then you're in all sorts of distressing and potentially embarrassing mayhem. But the kitchen and the waiters had managed to get through service running written orders up and down the stairs the nineteenth-century way, though a lot of complimentary glasses of Champagne were handed out during lunch and a lot of bills torn up. But the staff had done their best and kept their heads.

More congratulations: someone's got married. There are photos and a card to be signed in the staff dining room.

Now special changes to the menu, changes to the plating and the serving of dishes. There's a lot to remember – a cup of tea takes seven different items – then there's the seating. The floor manager goes through who's who and where they are, what they like, what they don't. This one will want a copy of the *Telegraph*, don't wait to be asked; this one a bottle of water on the table (sparkling), extra sugar with his coffee; this one is lactose-intolerant – mention milk products hidden in anything she orders – and that's that.

Except a last note on uniforms. There are too many bad shoes in the restaurant. Shirts tucked in, please.

THE CROISSANT

This recipe calls for a *poolish*, which is a yeast-based starter dough. The fermentation of the *poolish* yields a product with good keeping qualities and a better flavour. If you can only find dried yeast, use twice as much in each case.

Makes about 12

For the poolish
100g strong white (bread) flour
100ml water
2g fresh yeast

For the dough
150g plain flour
150g strong white (bread) flour
48g sugar
8g salt
1 egg, plus 1 more for the egg wash
55ml milk, plus a little more for the egg wash
20g fresh yeast
30g butter

For the turning
200g block of butter, well-chilled

At least a day ahead, make the *poolish* by mixing all the ingredients in a bowl. Cover and store at room temperature for 12 hours, or in the refrigerator for 24 hours to allow it to ferment slightly.

Place the *poolish* carefully into a mixing bowl, then cover with the flours, followed by the rest of the dough ingredients. Mix for 6 minutes at low speed, then 8 minutes at medium speed, until it forms a firm dough (ideally with a base temperature of 24 °C). Leave to prove for 50 minutes to 1 hour at cool room temperature.

Knock back the risen dough, then chill for 1–1½ hours.

Remove the dough and the block of butter for turning from the refrigerator and allow to warm a little. At the proper temperature, the dough will be fairly firm. The butter will be firm enough not to make your hands greasy but soft enough not to crack when bent.

Stretch the dough out into a large square (roughly 25cm). Bash the block of butter with the rolling pin until it is about the same thickness as the dough and half its width – it should fit into the centre. Place the butter on the dough and fold the dough up over it so that it overlaps on top, forming a large packet. Pinch the edges.

Roll the dough out into a long, thin rectangle and trim the short edges where you can see the butter. Fold in about one-sixth of it from one end, then bring in the other end to meet that but overlap it slightly. Press to seal, then chill again for at least half an hour. After this, roll it out at right angles to the last roll and repeat the folding. Chill again.

Roll the chilled dough out to a 40 x 32cm rectangle, 5mm thick. Mark it lengthwise into halves, then crosswise into 8cm rectangles. Mark each of the 8 rectangles across diagonally. Cut out each of the 16 triangles. Cut a little notch into the base of each triangle (this will allow the dough to spread sideways when you start rolling it into a croissant shape). Run each of the rectangles between thumb and forefinger to stretch it slightly, until it is about half as long again, then roll it up into a croissant shape.

Brush the croissants lightly with an egg wash made by beating the second egg with a little milk. Leave them to prove, ideally at a cool room temperature (21–23°C), for about 1½ hours, or until they have roughly doubled in size.

Preheat the oven to 190°C or gas mark 5. Brush the croissants once more with egg wash and bake for about 12 minutes until crisp and golden brown. Cool before serving.

When you can't make your own…

This recipe would be a challenge for even the most expert of home cooks. In reality, you will probably use commercially made croissants. Buy only the best 'all-butter' croissants. To reheat them, remember you are only *reheating them. Do not attempt to cook them; they are as fragile as the air that makes them rise. Place them into a cold oven and set at 80°C (or your very lowest gas mark setting); heat for 10 minutes.*

Pain au Chocolat

Makes 12–15

flour for dusting
1 recipe quantity chilled croissant dough (see pages 32–3)
240g good-quality dark chocolate (50–60% cocoa solids will give the
best flavour), cut into thick bars about 6–7cm long, each weighing
about 10g
beaten egg, to glaze

On a lightly floured surface, roll out the croissant dough into a 40 x 36cm rectangle to a thickness of 4mm. Cut into rectangles 8cm wide and 12cm long.

Place 1 bar of chocolate at both the top and bottom of each rectangle. Roll the dough towards you, enveloping the 2 bars of chocolate in the centre.

Place on baking trays with the seam on the bottom to avoid the *pain au chocolat* unrolling during proving and baking.

Glaze lightly with beaten egg and leave to prove for about 1¼ hours at warm room temperature (24°C).

Preheat the oven to 170–180°C or gas mark 3½–4. Glaze the pastries lightly with beaten egg for a second time and bake for 12–13 minutes until golden brown.

Allow to cool slightly before serving.

Pain au Beurre Normande Salé

This is effectively a *pain au chocolat*, but with salted butter replacing the chocolate. The salted butter enriches the croissant dough, while the sugar adds a sweet crunch.

Makes 12–15

flour for dusting
1 recipe quantity chilled croissant dough (see pages 32–3)
300g good-quality salted butter, cut into long, thick sticks about 6–7cm,
  each weighing about 20g
beaten egg, to glaze
demerara sugar, for sprinkling

Prepare the croissant dough as for the *pain au chocolat* on page 35, cutting it into 8 x 12cm rectangles.

Place a stick of salted butter at the top of each rectangle. Roll the dough towards you as for the *pain au chocolat* to enclose the butter. Place seam-side down on a baking tray.

Glaze lightly with beaten egg and chill briefly to firm up the pastry slightly.

Using a sharp knife, make 5–6 parallel cuts on the top of the pastry roll. Leave to prove for about 1¼ hours at warm room temperature (24°C).

Preheat the oven to 170–180°C or gas mark 3½–4. Glaze the pastries lightly with beaten egg for a second time, then sprinkle the tops with demerara sugar. Bake for 12–13 minutes until golden brown.

Allow to cool slightly before serving.

Choux au Fromage

Although these *choux* are offered in the bar during breakfast service, they are also available at lunch and dinner. They are a wonderful accompaniment to an aperitif.

Makes 10 large pieces or 30 small ones

> *125ml water*
> *125ml milk*
> *125g butter*
> *6g (or about 1 teaspoon) salt*
> *125g plain flour*
> *6 large eggs*
> *200g Emmental cheese, diced, plus more for grating*
> *5g (or about 2 teaspoons) black pepper*
> *1–2g freshly grated nutmeg*

In a saucepan, bring the water, the milk, butter and salt to the boil.

Add the flour all at once and beat with a wooden spoon over the heat for a full minute.

Remove from the heat and continue to stir for a minute to allow it to cool slightly.

Place the paste into a mixing bowl and beat with a mixer on medium speed. Whisk the mix for a minute to cool slightly, thereby avoiding the immediate 'cooking' of the eggs as they are added. Continue to beat the paste and begin incorporating the eggs one by one. Once all the eggs have been added, cover the surface with cling film and leave to cool.

Preheat the oven to 180°C or gas mark 4. Add the diced Emmental, pepper and nutmeg to the dough paste and stir well.

Spoon the paste onto baking sheets (30g each for mini pieces, 100g for larger pieces) and grate a little more Emmental on the top of each piece.

Bake for about 20–25 minutes, or until they are a golden-brown colour.

BRIOCHE

Being sweet and light, yet cakey, buttery and rich with eggs, brioche has long been a favourite for breakfast in place of bread or croissants. It can be served as it is or sliced and toasted to great effect, and with both sweet and savoury accompaniments.

Makes 6 pieces

125g plain flour
125g strong bread flour
35g caster sugar
5g (or a generous teaspoon) salt
12g fresh yeast
2 eggs
50ml milk
150g butter, diced

Start making the brioche the day before you want to bake it. Place the flours, sugar, salt and yeast in the mixing bowl of a food processor.

In another mixing bowl, combine the eggs and the milk, then add two-thirds of this egg mixture to the dry ingredients in the processor.

Mix for 8 minutes on the lowest speed, then continue for 20 minutes on medium speed, adding the diced butter a little at a time, ensuring that it is fully incorporated at each stage before adding any more.

Slowly add the remaining egg mixture, a little at a time, until the dough comes away from the sides of the bowl. The dough should be smooth, elastic and have a visible sheen. Its final temperature should be around 18°C (it should feel quite cold). If it is too hot, chill it until roughly that temperature. Then form the dough into a ball, cover and allow to prove for 1½–2 hours at room temperature.

Turn out the dough onto a floured surface and roll it out into a rectangle about twice as long as it is wide. With its length going from left to right in front of you, fold in the left-hand third and then fold in the right-hand third on top of that, pushing down firmly. Turn the dough 90 degrees, roll it out again, then fold in thirds in the same way once more, pushing down firmly to remove any excess gases that have developed. Cover fully and refrigerate overnight.

Next day, divide and shape it into 6 small loaves, then leave these to prove on baking sheets at 23–26°C (warm room temperature) for 1½–2 hours.

Preheat the oven to 180°C or gas mark 4 and bake the brioche for 20–25 minutes until well risen and golden. Cool on a wire rack.

Note

The classic brioche à tête *('brioche with a head'), made from one small ball of dough set atop a larger ball, is also known as Parisian brioche. When baked in a characteristic fluted mould, it is called Nanterre brioche. The plaited version, usually flavoured with rum, brandy or orange-flower water, is typical of the Vendée.*

Brioche with sugar is an Italian invention; derivations include festive treats such as pannetone *and* pan d'oro.

DOUBLE CHOCOLATE BRIOCHE

Makes 12 pieces

> 1 recipe quantity basic brioche, folded and chilled (see page 40)
> 150g chocolate chips
> chocolate shavings to decorate

> **For the crème patissière**
> 125ml milk
> 100ml double cream
> ½ vanilla pod, split
> 1 egg
> 40g caster sugar
> 20g instant custard powder

To make the *crème patissière*, combine the milk, cream and vanilla in a saucepan and bring to the boil. Combine the egg, sugar and custard powder in a large heatproof mixing bowl, whisking until smooth. Pour half the boiling liquid onto the cold mixture and immediately whisk until smooth. Return this mixture to the remaining boiling milk and cream, place back on the heat and continue whisking briskly until the *crème patissière* begins to boil. Remove from the heat. Put the finished mixture on a tray or plate, cover with cling film and allow to cool.

On a lightly floured surface, roll out the brioche dough to a thickness of about 3mm and shape into a rectangle about 50 x 25cm. Spread this with the *crème patissière*, discarding the vanilla pod, leaving clear borders of about 5mm at the sides. Sprinkle the *crème patissière* liberally with chocolate chips.

Roll one long edge towards the centre, then do the same with the opposite edge. Cut this 'double cylinder' across into pieces about 1cm wide. Allowing 2 pieces per portion, twist each one and join them at the centre, flat-sides down, in a Maltese-cross shape. Leave to prove for 1–1½ hours at warm room temperature (about 24°C) until light to the touch.

Preheat the oven to 175°C or gas mark 3½ and bake the brioches for 10–12 minutes. Cool and garnish with chocolate shavings or more chocolate chips.

EGGS

It's 6.55 a.m. Five minutes to go. Check that the menus are correct. Check that each table has one. Check your menu pads for specials and new ingredients. Check your station has enough teaspoons. For reasons known only to the cutlery sprite, teaspoons are the convertible currency of all dining rooms. There are never enough, however many there are. In abstract monetarist economics they will never be where you need them. There must be a secret freedom train for teaspoons, smuggling them out of dining rooms into a promised land where nothing needs stirring, and no one eats yoghurt.

Down in the kitchen, the breakfast brigade has been preparing for an hour. Today there are three of them to see to the entire service: an Australian breakfast chef and her two *sous-chefs*, a Malian and a Californian with an infectious weatherproof grin.

The African *sous-chef* is the egg man today: anything that's backed out of a hen is his responsibility. He beats a bucket of hollandaise.
Has it ever split on him? Once.
'I was so surprised they could do that. Why would they split on me?'

Hollandaise has only recently become a comfortable and clubbable member of the international breakfast club. It comes with the eggs

Benedict, a dish of the industrial metropolis. Whereas most breakfast foods have humble origins in private kitchens, eggs Benedict was born in public catering, like *Viennoiserie*. In the *Larousse Gastronomique*, the encyclopaedia of classical dishes, there are 250 dishes prefaced 'eggs' which don't include the 123 omelettes or uncounted scrambled-egg recipes or the single entry for a Scotch egg (how out of place do you think a Scotch egg feels in the *Larousse Gastronomique*?). But there isn't a recipe for eggs Benedict. (There is one for eggs Bénédictine: hard-boiled eggs served cold and covered in a white sauce. It didn't catch on.)

Benedict comes from America: from New York, the city of public eating. And there are two versions of the story of its origin. The first comes from a cookbook called *The Epicurean*, written by Charles Ranhoffer, the chef of Delmonico's, sometimes credited as being the first restaurant in Manhattan. He says a regular patron called Mrs Le Grande Benedict, finding nothing she liked on the menu for lunch, asked for something new, and chef came up with eggs Benedict, which he called *eig à la Benedict*. This doesn't have the ring of voracity. I don't trust Ranhoffer; he's a chef – they can lie. And Mrs Le Grande Benedict is a character from Damon Runyon or P. G. Wodehouse: not a real person.

The other creation story is from The Waldorf, the hotel that gave us the salad (though why anyone wanted to make Waldorf salad twice is beyond me; it's boring and nasty in equal measure). The Waldorf at the turn of the century was famous for its chef, Oscar Tschirky. *The New Yorker* magazine ran an interview with a cove called Lemuel Benedict – now that *is* a proper New York name. He took a monster hangover to The Waldorf and ordered hot buttered toast, crisp bacon, two poached eggs and a hooker of hollandaise. The chef was intrigued, substituted English muffin for toast, Canadian bacon (back) for crisp (streaky) and there you are: a legend was born. This is how cooks make food: they see something, taste something, and then tinker with it.

The thing that really convinces me, though, is the hangover. Hangovers make people eat desperate things – prairie oysters, for instance. Eggs Benedict is still the best morning-after dish ever invented.

The only thing about this story that niggles is the 'hooker' of hollandaise. In this context, what's a hooker? Well, of course I know what a hooker is. Perhaps Lemuel asked for eggs and bacon, the hooker and hollandaise; the sauce was to go on the girl?

Eggs Benedict came to this country along with a new meal. It's incredibly difficult to invent a new meal. For over 10,000 years as a species we have eaten every eight hours, sticking a new sit-down knife and fork meal in the middle somewhere. Tinkering with the timing of humanity is really fundamental, but in America all new things are possible, and they conflated two ancient repasts and came up with brunch.

Eggs Benedict is the star, the Marilyn Monroe of brunch. It is an indulgence dish invariably prefixed with 'Oh, I shouldn't, really'. It's the addition of the rich, unctuous hollandaise to the perfectly catholic and unimpeachably healthy Anglo-Saxon poached egg and bacon that makes it feel greedy. And then there's the option of having one or two eggs, but a single Benedict is a sorry thing; a double is gastronomy. I always thought they should call the single The Benedict and the double The Benedict and Beatrice.

The origins of hollandaise are even more problematic. It's generally thought to be French, but only because the French codified sauces and sauce-making, thereby annexing a lot of European thickened juices, gravies and stocks that have been cooked round the Continent for thousands of years. Bernaise is a warm variation of mayonnaise, which is as old as olive oil, and that makes it older than farming. But French

cuisine was laid down in the eighteenth century and was principally remarkable for its original use of sauces.

Hollandaise is one of the five basics, made with butter instead of olive oil. There is a recipe from 1758, but it doesn't include an egg yolk and does have flour, so it's really more of a roux or a white sauce. *De verstandige kok* – a book written in 1683 that really ought to be about group sex but is, in fact, Dutch for 'The Sensible Cook' – lists a sauce of butter, eggs and vinegar to be served with eels, but there's no method. And the name 'hollandaise' is almost certainly from Holland, which was famous for the quality of its sweet butter and eggs. Occasionally it's called Dutch sauce, but I have a theory (less than a theory, really; more a suggestion) that hollandaise in its recognizable particular form is actually German.

It became commonly fashionable in the 1730s at the time when German farmers perfected the complex and ruinously expensive business of growing *Spargel*, or white asparagus. Germans were besotted and addicted to it. They still are. The *Spargel* season is the time to avoid in Germany;

there is nothing else to eat. Unlike everybody else in the world, they seem never to tire of it, and the faint but insistent aroma of asparagus pee lingers everywhere. Hollandaise goes particularly well with asparagus; it's inconceivable that they ate one without the other.

Hollandaise sauce is considered tricky to make, but it's actually a simple mixture of physics and thermodynamics. The physics is your arm, the thermodynamics is that if it gets too warm, it melts and separates. A chemist once did an experiment to see how much mayonnaise he could make from a single egg yolk (the principle is the same with hollandaise). He never found out. They stopped after four gallons. The quality of egg yolk is mysterious and mystical and something you might want to ponder over breakfast.

After he has finished the hollandaise and set it aside on a bain-marie, the breakfast chef plops eggs into seething water to poach. Poached eggs are a boon for restaurants. They can be made in advance and warmed when needed without suffering; in fact, some maintain that they're best if the eggs are a couple of days old because the whites of very, very fresh eggs don't set properly.

An egg is the most perfect and important universal food item. They say no egg from an animal is poisonous, but just don't take my word for it. When we say an egg, we mean a chicken egg. Chickens came to Europe 1,500 years ago. There are no mentions of chickens in Homer, although he writes a lot about food, and they managed to get to England only 700 years later, along with the Romans. Which came first is the wrong question. The chicken became the most populous bird in the world, not because it made deep-fried nuggets or buffalo wings or chicken soup, but because it had the sense to produce eggs. It's the egg that has made the chicken welcome round the world and valuable to every cuisine.

Eggs are twelve percent protein, twelve percent fat: a perfect symmetry. In a month, this kitchen will serve over 12,000 of them poached, scrambled, fried, boiled and in omelettes; eggs in French toast, hollandaise, in pastry, in bread, in glazes; eggs in ice cream, in custard, in mousses and hard-boiled on the bar.

THINGS YOU SHOULD
KNOW ABOUT EGGS

~ Ensure that eggs to be boiled have been removed from the refrigerator and allowed to come to room temperature. If this is not possible, then you will have to add one or two minutes to the cooking time. Timing is not the only issue here, though; if chilled eggs are put into hot water, their shells are likely to crack. You can try tempering the eggs by putting them in a bowl of hot water from the tap for a couple of minutes.

~ VERY fresh eggs can be problematic for the cook: they can be difficult to beat to a foam and, if boiled, can be very fiddly to shell.

~ Buy eggs from a reputable retailer, who you can be certain will have ensured that they have been transported and stored at the correct temperature (below 20°C).

~ The colour of the eggshell is only an indication of the variety of bird from which it came and is otherwise completely unrelated to either its flavour or nutritional value.

~ Eggs are now classified as small (53g or less; previously 5, 6 and 7), medium (53–63g; previously 3, 4 and 5), large (63–73g; previously 1, 2 and 3), and very large (73g or more; previously 0 and 1).

~ Wash your hands before and after handling eggs, but do not wash your eggs, as this removes a natural film that prevents bacteria from entering the porous shell.

~ Discard any dirty or cracked eggs.

~ It is recommended that eggs be stored in the refrigerator.

~ Remember that eggshells are porous, so store eggs separately from other foods, either in their box or in a sealed compartment or container, if you don't want them to pick up odours. Eggs may, of course, use this property to their advantage, taking on such fabulous aromas as that of the truffle.

~ To ensure that an egg is fresh, place it carefully in a deep, clear glass and then fill the glass with water. If the egg shows signs of floating upwards, then the air bubble inside the shell (which develops as the egg dries out) is quite large and the egg is quite likely to be stale or even rotten.

THE PERFECTLY BOILED EGG

Boiled eggs are perhaps the most strenuous test of the quality and taste of an egg. The shell, although porous, is still the armour and encasement of this primary food.

~ Bring a suitably sized pan of water to a full but gentle simmer. Adding a splash of vinegar in a ratio of 1 part vinegar to 10 parts water affects the ease with which you can remove the shell from the eggs.

~ Gently lower the eggs into the water using a slotted spoon. If cooking more than one or two eggs, it may be a good idea to lower them into the water in a wire basket so that they all start cooking at the same time. Adjust the heat to bring the eggs to the boil quickly, then readjust to a simmer.

~ After 1–1½ minutes of simmering for small eggs, 2 minutes for medium and 3 for large, the whites will be firm but not yet fully set and the yolk still runny – what the French term *mollet*. Such eggs can be shelled with care and served or used as a poached egg.

~ Many people prefer their eggs medium-soft or even medium-hard; the former requires another 30 seconds, while the latter needs up to a minute of further cooking. If cooking many eggs which require different degrees of cooking, simply remove them with a slotted spoon at the correct time.

~ After 4 minutes for small, 5 minutes for medium, and 6 for large, the whites will will be firmly set and the yolks will be set but still soft and tender.

~ After 8 minutes for small eggs, 9 for medium, 10 for large, both the whites and yolks will be fully set – ideal for slicing or chopping as a garnish. This is about as far as you need to boil an egg, even for a pregnant lady.

~ As soon as the eggs have reached the required stage of cooking, plunge them into cold water to stop any further cooking.

~ To shell a boiled egg, roll it firmly but gently on a hard surface to crack evenly all over. It is then easier to remove the membrane underneath the shell. It is best not to shell the eggs until they are to be used, otherwise they will dry out.

THE PERFECTLY SCRAMBLED EGG

~ Check the use-by date of the eggs as, if they are not that fresh, adding any milk or water to them may make the results too watery. Ideally have the eggs at room temperature (or temper them in some warm water from the tap for a couple of minutes, if they are straight from the fridge).

~ In a mixing bowl, lightly beat 2–3 eggs per person (depending on their size) with salt and pepper to taste. You can – if your eggs are fresh enough – add a couple of tablespoons of water or milk or cream at this stage. As it turns to steam, the water is said to lighten the result; the milk or cream can make the eggs creamier, but purists say that the cooked milk solids toughen the results and can add an unwelcome flavour.

~ Gently heat 15–30g butter per person in a heavy-based (preferably non-stick) pan until melted. Try to match the size of the pan to the quantity of egg; you don't want too high a proportion of the mix to be in contact with the bottom, or the eggs will cook too rapidly. A 20cm pan is ideal for 3–4 eggs; 25cm for 6–8 eggs.

~ Add the eggs and briefly increase the heat, then lower it again after a count of ten. Start stirring the eggs as they turn opaque. Continue to cook gently, stirring fairly constantly (leaving intervals between stirs allows the formation of larger curds, which some people prefer) until the eggs are just short of the ideal creamy texture and are not in any way set.

~ Remove the pan immediately from the heat, still stirring, as you want the residual heat in the pan to finish the cooking of the eggs. A spoonful or two of double cream stirred in at this stage not only adds texture but will also lower the temperature and help stop the eggs overcooking. If you think it necessary, you can also put the bottom of the pan in some cold water.

~ Season again, if necessary, serve and eat immediately.

Note
One way of ensuring really fluffy scrambled eggs is to beat an extra egg white per person until it stands in soft peaks, then fold that into the whole-egg mixture before cooking.

THE PERFECTLY POACHED EGG

~ Eggs need ideally to be really fresh for good poached eggs, so that the egg keeps its shape in the water. If your eggs aren't that fresh, one good trick is to pop them in the freezer for about 15 minutes, so that the whites get much more viscous.

~ Bring a large, heavy, shallow pan of water to a steady gentle simmer and add 1 or 2 dessertspoons of distilled vinegar. As with boiled eggs, the amount of vinegar placed in the water will allow a 'tight' form and presentable shape: the white will not wander or separate from the yolk. Do not add salt, as this will toughen the egg. The best vinegar to use is a distilled clear vinegar. Avoid all malt or herb vinegars as the flavour will dilute the flavour of the egg and could also be transferred to it.

~ Crack the eggs into heatproof teacups or saucers, then lower into the water and slip them out onto the simmering surface. Once they are all in (don't poach more than 4 eggs at a time or they reduce the water temperature too much), cover with a lid and leave undisturbed for 3 minutes. It is important that the water is still moving; this stops the eggs from sinking to the bottom or cooking unevenly and will facilitate their removal. Some people advocate swirling the water around in a vortex to help shape the eggs, but this only works for 1 or 2 eggs, and it shouldn't be necessary if the eggs are fresh enough and the handling and cooking sufficiently gentle.

~ At the end of this time, check on the eggs. If they are properly cooked, the whites will all be opaque and the yolks just visible through a veil of white. If not, put the lid back on for another 20 seconds or so until the eggs are cooked. Because the contents of the eggs are in more direct contact with the hot water, the timing of poached eggs is not as affected by the size of the eggs as in the case of boiling.

~ Lift the eggs out quickly with a perforated spoon. If not serving them immediately, carefully place them into a bowl of iced water to stop the cooking process. If serving them straight away, a quick dip in fresh warm water can help lessen any vinegar flavour, if that is important to you.

~ Once they are cold, you can, if you like, lift the eggs carefully out of the water and neaten their appearance by trimming off any ragged bits of white.

~ If necessary, the poached eggs will keep in the bowl of cold water for several days. When you are ready to use them, just lower them into another pan of gently simmering water for up to 2 minutes to reheat.

EGGS BENEDICT

Serves 2

> 4 eggs, poached (see page 57)
> 4 muffins, toasted
> 4 slices of ham
> good pinch of chopped chives
> good pinch of cayenne pepper

> **For the hollandaise sauce** *(makes about 250ml)*
> 4 tablespoons white-wine vinegar
> 2 shallots, coarsely chopped
> 10 peppercorns
> 175g butter, cut into cubes
> 3 egg yolks
> juice of ½ lemon
> salt

First make the sauce: put the vinegar, shallots and peppercorns in a saucepan and bring to the boil, then continue to boil until reduced by about two-thirds. Strain this reduction into a glass bowl.

Clarify the butter by melting it in another heavy pan over a gentle heat. Skim the surface until only clear liquid remains. Remove from the heat and allow it to settle and cool until tepid, then carefully tip out the clarified butter into a clean bowl, leaving any solid residue behind.

Place a round heatproof bowl over a pan of simmering water. Add the egg yolks and the reduction. Beat the mixture over the heat until it forms a smooth, thick, pale mass.

Remove from the heat and whisk vigorously, adding enough of the clarified butter to make a thick and creamy sauce. It is important to whisk in the same direction all the time. This technique takes muscle and commitment, probably even a few trips to the gym. The reason why is to make a lovely, fluffy hollandaise sauce. It may not happen the first time, but practice will achieve fantastic results.

If the sauce should separate at any point, beat a fresh egg yolk with a spoonful of water in a clean bowl, then whisk the separated sauce into that; it should magically come back to a smooth sauce. Adjust the flavour with a little lemon juice and salt to taste. Keep warm.

While the eggs are poaching, toast the muffins, first removing a thin slice from the top of each. Keep the grill on.

Butter the toasted muffins and then arrange the ham on top of them. Press a good thumb- or spoon-print into the middle of each muffin to give the eggs a neat hollow. Put them back under the grill briefly to warm up.

When the eggs are cooked, drain them well and season with salt. Place them in their prepared hollows and ladle over the hollandaise. Sprinkle with cayenne pepper and chives to garnish.

Variations
Eggs Arlington is simply a variation on eggs Benedict, in which the ham is replaced with long slices of smoked salmon formed into rings to receive the poached eggs. Eggs Florentine is a vegetarian version of this type of dish, in which the ham or smoked salmon is replaced with some buttered cooked spinach.

THE PERFECTLY FRIED EGG

~ Place a heavy frying pan, preferably non-stick and with a tight-fitting lid, over a medium heat and add a knob of butter and a drop or two of olive oil (to help prevent the butter burning – or you could use clarified butter: see page 58). As the butter melts, swirl it around the bottom of the pan.

~ Either crack the eggs directly into their own space in the pan, or first break them into a cup and pour them in from that. Lower the heat to halfway between low and medium.

~ For the classic fried egg, also known as 'sunny-side up', cover the pan tightly and cook for 3–5 minutes. The white of the egg should be firmly set and lightly coloured around the edges while the yolk should be cooked on its underside but still runny on top, with the lightest of translucent films over it.

~ If you want your egg yolk more cooked without overcooking the white, go for the 'over-easy' option. After 3 minutes, carefully position a spatula or fish slice under the egg and flip it over. Cook very briefly on this second side, uncovered.

~ Season and serve immediately.

Note

There are other ways of getting a more cooked yolk without flipping the egg. If you are frying lots of eggs, or frying the eggs with something fatty like bacon and have a good deal of butter or other fat in the pan, then you can baste the yolks with the hot fat from the side of the pan. Alternatively, after about 2 minutes of cooking as above, drop a spoonful or two of water onto a bare part of the pan base and cover the pan immediately. The resultant steam will cook the egg-yolk tops in the remaining time.

THE PERFECT OMELETTE

Omelettes at The Wolseley are very simple: only eggs and seasoning are used. The best are made by cooking with gas as you have more control over the heat. If using an electric hob, be prepared to take the pan off the heat as necessary.

~ Beat the eggs together, but not too much, or they will be heavier and more watery. Pour into a very clean and dry pan coated with just a film of melted butter. It should be hot enough for the butter to have stopped foaming, but should not be smoking.

~ As the curds cook, use a spatula to draw the outer edges into the middle, allowing uncooked egg to flow into contact with the hot pan. Add any seasoning at this stage. Any earlier, and the salt will cause the eggs to toughen and become watery.

~ The aim is to get a nicely set and coloured underside and a top that is still just slightly liquid, so that the finished omelette will be what the French call *baveuse*, or 'dribbling', when you dig an impatient fork into it. When sufficiently cooked, add any filling and fold one-half of the omelette over the other.

~ As well as the inner consistency, there are two types of finish, depending on the degree of overall cooking: the golden brown and the pale, light and fluffy.

~ There are many other variations on these final stages. The omelette can be folded inward in thirds, or have one-third folded in and then the omelette tipped out on a plate to fold the remaining third underneath, producing a long, narrow omelette.

~ When plated, allow your omelette to stand for a minute or two, depending on the temperature of the room.

Note

If you do not possess a well-seasoned pan (i.e. well-greased and heat-ready) use a non-stick pan. Remember, though, that the temperature of the pan is key in order not to colour the omelette and allow it to remain baveuse *on the inside. A 20cm pan is recommended for a three-egg omelette.*

It is also very important to only use butter. The marriage of the butter and the eggs is paramount. Those with butter allergies, of course, should use a suitable margarine or other non-dairy spread.

OMELETTE ARNOLD BENNETT

Serves 2

250g smoked haddock
250ml milk
½ onion
1½ bay leaves
1 clove
125ml hollandaise sauce (see page 58)
4 tablespoons double cream
8 large eggs plus 2 extra egg yolks
clarified butter (see page 58), for frying
chopped chives, to serve

Poach the haddock in the gently simmering milk along with the onion, bay leaves and clove until the flesh flakes readily: about 5 minutes. Remove the haddock, flake the fish into a large mixing bowl and leave to cool.

Mix the hollandaise sauce, cream and the extra egg yolks. Set aside.

Preheat a hot grill.

Heat a little clarified butter in a non-stick omelette pan. Whisk 3 eggs and make an omelette as described on page 63 – but don't cook it through.

Tip out of the pan onto a heatproof serving plate and spoon over half of the cooked haddock. Spoon over half the hollandaise mix and place under the grill until it begins to glaze. Make the second omelette while that is glazing and finish it in the same way.

Sprinkle with chives and serve.

FRENCH TOAST

The original version of this dish in France – *pain perdu*, or 'lost bread' – was a way of using up stale French bread, which, of course, dries within a day.

Serves 4

> *clarified butter (see page 58), for frying*
> *8 thickish slices of brioche (see page 40)*
> *icing sugar, for dusting*
>
> ### For the batter
> *3 large eggs*
> *4 tablespoons double cream*
> *20g caster sugar*
> *freshly grated nutmeg*
> *ground cinnamon*

First make the batter: in a wide, shallow bowl, mix the eggs, cream and sugar together, adding nutmeg and cinnamon to taste.

Heat some clarified butter in a frying pan. Just cover the base of the pan, and only add more butter if you need it; otherwise you'll have a greasy, soggy bread.

Dip the slices of brioche into the batter, shake off any excess and gently fry in the clarified butter until golden-brown on both sides.

Remove from the pan and quickly drain on some kitchen paper. Serve sprinkled with icing sugar.

ENGLISH
BREAKFAST

The breakfast kitchen has three salamanders (like your grill, only fiercer), two hotplates and a couple of warming ovens; it's concentrated work in a small area. On the other side of the oven, the Californian does cooked breakfasts, pork in all its wonder and variety. These two cooks – the Californian and the Malian – are an example of the difference between involvement and commitment. The chicken is involved in breakfast, the pig committed.

The Wolseley may have a distinctly Viennese, cosmopolitan air, it may have New World innovation and comfort, but there is on the menu one thing that you will find only on this island. While croissants, cappuccinos and eggs Benedict have gracefully colonized the mornings of the world, very few other nations have felt the need or the desire to open their mouths and arteries to the Full English Breakfast. But you couldn't have any sort of café here that set its table with a knife and fork that didn't boast the complete plateful. There are many reasons why the Full English hasn't caught on in the rest of the world: the bore of making it, for a start. It's not complicated, but it is fiddly; getting everything all fried and onto the plate at once is tricky. Good English Breakfasts have to be made individually, and if you make one at home, unless you dispensed with the roof or have a crematorium's extraction system, your kitchen's going to look like the set of a Sherlock Holmes film, and smell like the fire-bombing of Dresden.

That's not really the reason. Foreigners look askance and pudgy-cheeked at the Full English because of its cacophony of meat: the abundance and repetition of its piggy-ness. Very few cultures want to eat that much body for breakfast. They tend to concentrate instead on cereals, carbohydrates and fruit. To be confronted with this great carnivorous autopsy first thing is really more than the denizens of lesser nations can stomach.

There is something particularly mountainous and bloody-minded about the chew-a-thon of an English Breakfast that appeals specifically to the

Anglo-Saxon. We look at the plate with a smile of recognition. It is a mirror of ourselves. If in some way all nations become advertisements for their diet, then the English have been misnamed by the Continent as *les rosbifs*. They are, in fact, 'The Full English': the diverse and contradictory bits of fortified and preserved pig meat that are different, but all part of the same animal.

The final reason most foreigners sensibly don't want to broach our breakfast is because as you finish, you are overtaken with the leaden desire, almost the imperative need, to go back to bed again.

I once went out with an Italian for breakfast. He looked at his plate with wide-eyed astonishment.

'Aha,' he said. 'This is where dinner went? People I'm staying with gave me hot cheese on bread with a cup of tea last night. That was obviously breakfast. Of course, never seeing the sunshine, you must all lose track of your meals.'

The Wolseley's English Breakfast comprises bacon, sausage, baked beans, tomato, black pudding and mushrooms with eggs: fried, poached or scrambled. Personally, I think the beans are *de trop* and an unnecessary addition from a trucker's motorway café, and there should be fried bread. Beans in tomato sauce are, anyway, a recent addition from America, a cowboy concoction canned in the great processing revolution of the nineteenth century. The black pudding is the smaller Lancashire variety, not the oaty wagonwheels of Scotland and Ireland, or the gory and delicious *boudin* of France.

No one really knows the origin of black pudding; it must be as old as slaughter. There is certainly mention in Homer of stomach filled with blood and fat and roasted on a fire, so Achilles ate it. Sausage is much the same, buried in the guts of antiquity. The word comes from the Latin for 'to salt or preserve', and what is particular to British sausage is that it's not made as a means of extending the life of small, otherwise inedible bits of pork. Everywhere else in Europe, sausages tend to be salami. The Germans made a number of *Wurst*s which they grill or fry, but none of them have the fresh, piggy, unctuous brilliance of a British banger. The Italians make a half-hearted thing tied up with string that they eat with beans, but their heart's not in it. Sausage is not something any of us can claim to be impartial about. We are forever indebted and engaged to the sausages of our childhood. The English are all crusaders on a quest to find the perfect sausage that will resemble the mystical blackened and grisly deliciousness of childhood picnics. My advice to the twenty-five nations serving in The Wolseley and the dozens of nations eating there is never get into an argument about sausages with an Englishman. There is no gain nor end to it. (For what it's worth, my pet gripe and grizzle is that they don't seem to burst the way they once did: the peculiar pleasure of a sausage is in its dysfunction. When it goes wrong, it splits its side and becomes crisp and charcoaled with a great wound in its belly.)

The true national treasure in The Full English is, though, the bacon. It will come as a surprise to even the most jingoistic new Brit foodie to discover that the English actually invented bacon. True, the Germans have something they call *Speck* and the Italians *pancetta*, while the French eat a substance called *poitrine,* but none of these is salted on the bone and then sliced 'green' or mildly smoked and fried. All bacon around the world is made to English recipes. The Americans may foolishly think it comes from Canada, and the lion's share of ours does come from Denmark and Holland, but it's all English. The large white, or Yorkshire, pig, with its legs designed for York ham, is the bacon pig. The Danes invented the

Landrace with a long back to please English breakfast habits. A cross between the two is now the commercial pig of the bacon industry.

Bacon was the staple protein of the English rural working class from the eighteenth century, and the industrial working class in the nineteenth. A large proportion of the country lived off rashers of bacon, doorsteps of bread and cups of tea. It sustained the Empire for nearly 100 years.

If you've ever read old recipes and wondered what 'collops' were, they are rashers or slices of bacon. Most kitchens kept a large cast-iron frying pan permanently on the side of the hob. It was rarely washed: just occasionally drained of fat, which was kept in an earthenware jar beside the stove. Bacon dripping was spread on bread. Dripping and lard were the cooking fats of the English kitchen. Up until the Great War, bacon was dry-cured, but the demand from the army became so great that they began to brine-cure and injected the meat with salt water. The white scum that comes off mass-produced bacon is the last, lingering legacy of the Somme. The Wolseley will serve 15,000 rashers of bacon a month.

The Californian cook juggles his ingredients, the Malian slides the eggs in the nick of time onto the plates under the lights of the pass. In front, the Australian chef is preparing French toast in an egg mix and making pancakes. Behind her are six dumbwaiters.

The American chef prods the fish cakes with his thumb, making a dent that's just enough to nestle a poached egg. This is all to come. Now they're quiet. Now they're waiting at their stations for the doors to open. Orders come down on the Remanco, or through a squeaky intercom; these are the kitchen's only connections to the daylight world.

When the restaurant's busy, the orders chatter out constantly. They're printed in duplicate, the chef reads them out and clips one half to the top of the pass, where it stays until it's transported heavenward.

'One double Benny. One English – hold the black pudding. One scrambled with smoked, toast on the side. One cheese omelette, well done; two pancakes. Where are the poached eggs for this?'

An overalled *plongeur* pushes a broom down the narrow aisle between the stations of gastronomy. The most dangerous thing in a kitchen isn't knives or fire or boiling oil; it's the floor. Wet, slimy, sticky – a sliver of potato or peel, or a box of crayfish can cause horrifying accidents. In kitchens they generally happen from the bottom up. The brush leaves long, grey streaks on the tiles; the chef points to a little pile of detritus lurking in a corner. Down behind him come two commis chefs carrying a couple of gallons of stock: the saffron oil on the surface shimmies and sulks, looking for the pot lip and the break for freedom.

The *plongeur*'s face is set in whitewashed, passive displeasure. He does his job with a slow resignation, moving to a different metronome than the rest of the kitchen. There is no point in hurrying if you're a cleaner. There is no end – no end to dirt and spills and washing-up.

The dishwasher's station is just beside the kitchen, a room of gravity-defying piles of aluminium, copper, pottery, steel and silver. If the kitchen is all about greenness, flesh, sunshine and life, then this is minerals and metal: a little room that is the antithesis of cooking and hospitality. The dishwasher hoses plates, half-eaten guilty waste scraped and sluiced into industrial bins. The air is full of chemical hot steam. It smells of sodden food and detergent and disinfectant and wet mops.

The washing-up areas of restaurants are new starts, hard-scrubbed beginnings that sluice away the old. They wash not just the plates, but the old cultures and politics, wars, famines, plagues, disasters, mistakes and bad luck from the people who work in them. These big sinks that you could drown in are baptistries of new life and faith for generations of dishwashers. They are the further shore of immigration. In these little rooms you can trace any ebb and surge of this country's new citizens.

After the war, Republican Spaniards and starving southern Italians came here to sing their communist songs over the half-eaten boiled bacon. Then from the fifties to the nineties, it was West Indians, Bengalis, Somalis and Nigerians, and now, briefly, slim-featured, pale-eyed Poles, all of them with the same contrary mixture of relief and resentment: a battened-in, taciturn, steely ambition.

Washer-up isn't a job with prospects; it doesn't lead to anything but more washing-up, more slippery floors, more rubbish bags. But it is also, in a restaurant, the job with the greatest prospects. This is the first step, the moment where the exhausted and penniless take a breath, grab a mouthful of someone's discarded steak, and step into a new life.

THE ENGLISH BREAKFAST

Serves 4

4 large, fat pork sausages
oil for frying and/or grilling
butter for frying and/or grilling and scrambling
8 rashers of rindless smoked back bacon
4 thick slices of black pudding, skinned
4 large ripe tomatoes, halved
4 large eggs, fried (see page 61), poached (see page 57) or scrambled (see page 55)
1 x 400g tin of baked beans
400g large chestnut mushrooms, sliced or halved if small
at least 8 slices of toast, to serve
brown sauce, to serve

Whatever methods you use for the meats and tomatoes – frying or grilling (The Wolseley favours grilling) – the order of cooking remains very much the same. Start with the sausages, followed by the bacon, then the black pudding, and finally, the tomatoes. Fry briskly in a little vegetable oil (tomato halves cut-side down) or grill under a moderate heat (brush the sausages and tomatoes lightly with oil). The sausages will need 10–15 minutes, turning them three or four times to brown them evenly. The bacon needs 5–6 minutes, turning it after 3–4 minutes. Start the tomatoes cooking with the bacon: they take longer than you might expect.

Start cooking the eggs (see page numbers, above). Put the black pudding on to cook and the beans to warm in a small pan, then sauté the mushrooms in a little butter and oil over a moderate-to-high heat, stirring frequently, until well-coloured and softened.

At the last minute, make the toast. Serve everything together on well-warmed plates, with the toast on the side. Brown sauce is *de rigueur*.

If you don't have enough big pans or a big enough grill, preheat a cool oven (150°C or gas mark 2) with a large ovenproof serving dish inside. Put items in that, uncovered, as they are cooked. You can also cook the meats and tomatoes in an oven preheated to 200°C or gas mark 6. The sausages will need 30–45 minutes, depending on size; the bacon and tomatoes about 15–20; the black pudding 10–15 minutes.

ITALIAN BREAKFAST

This version of a cooked breakfast is great to eat outside and can be prepared in advance – except, of course, for cooking the eggs.

Serves 2

1 loaf of ciabatta bread
150g ceps, fresh or frozen
200g cherry vine tomatoes
extra-virgin olive oil, to drizzle
sea salt and freshly ground black pepper
a knob of butter
flat-leaf parsley, chopped
¼ garlic clove, crushed
4 eggs

Cut the ciabatta in half lengthwise. Drizzle some olive oil onto each half to moisten, then grill the bread until it turns a light golden colour.

If using fresh ceps, check that they are clean, without too much of the forest floor still attached. Try not to wash them, however, as they will deteriorate.

Coat the cherry vine tomatoes in olive oil, then season with sea salt and freshly ground black pepper. Bake in a hot oven at 225°C or gas mark 7 for four minutes, just to blister the skins and lightly colour them.

Meanwhile, cook the ceps. Over a low heat, melt the butter with a splash of olive oil; using both avoids burning the ceps. Increase the heat gradually so that the mushrooms caramelize. Ceps cry out for high heat, and caramelization makes them taste meaty and rich. Season with a tiny touch of garlic and a teaspoon of chopped parsley, then sea salt and freshly ground black pepper to taste.

Cook the eggs to your personal preference and serve with the grilled ciabatta.

CRISPY BACON AND EGG ROLL

Serves 2

> *10 rashers of cooked streaky bacon*
> *A drizzle of vegetable oil*
> *1 small teaspoon of butter*
> *2 eggs*
> *2 floured 'burger' baps, cut in half*

Place the streaky bacon on a flat tray and under the grill of your oven. Grill for 2 minutes each side, or until golden.

Once the bacon is under the grill, fry the eggs. Warm a small frying pan on the stove. Drizzle a few drops of oil and the butter into the frying pan, crack the egg as close as possible to the base of the pan and slowly empty the shell so that you have a small fried egg. You may fry more than one egg at a time in the same pan. Be careful not to get the pan too hot, however, so that it doesn't splatter and burn.

Place the bacon onto the bread bap and then the egg onto the bacon. Leave the top of the bap resting to one side so that you can see the egg and not break the yolk until ready to eat.

Buying bacon

There are three different types of bacon: back, middle and streaky. Back is good for sandwiches, while streaky is best for cooked breakfasts. To prevent shrinkage, buy rindless bacon; it should be lightly smoked.

Bacon should not be too fatty, but the fat should be proportional to the meat content. Read the label, look at the rasher size and the thickness of the fat level, and whether or not there is a rind. Middle rashers are meatier, and need to be cooked carefully so as not to dry them out.

There are five different types of cure: traditional Wiltshire, sweet cure, smoked bacon, maple cure and dry cure (the simplest is with sea salt and brown sugar). The flavours of these range from smoked and salty to sweet and subtle.

HAGGIS AND DUCK EGG

Serves 2

vegetable oil, for frying
10g butter, for frying
2 slices of white bread, crusts cut off
1 x 400g haggis, cut into 15mm slices
4 duck eggs

For the sauce
50ml whisky
200ml beef or
   chicken stock
50ml brown sauce
20g butter, diced

Place a tray lined with kitchen paper to the side of the stove, so that the bread may be taken from the pan once cooked and can drain and stop any further colouring.

Heat the oil in a frying pan. Once it has started to ripple and gained heat, drop in the butter and wait until it melts. Place the bread into the pan and fry on each side until it turns a pale golden colour. Lift out the bread and place on the kitchen paper to drain.

Place the sliced haggis onto a piece of baking paper in the frying pan. Using baking paper will help to prevent sticking and make the slices easier to lift from the pan and place on the plate. Fry the haggis on the parchment, seasoning the slices as you turn them. Lift them out and place them on top of the bread. Leave for 30 seconds, then place the lot into the middle of a warm serving dish.

Carefully place the duck eggs into two pans coated with melted butter. Do not get the pans too hot, as the eggs will burst and blister. In cooking an egg, the first step is to coagulate the white, which needs very little heat; the yolk will take a little longer to cook. Gently lift the eggs out with a palate knife or spatula and place them on top of the haggis.

To make the sauce, pour the whisky into a small saucepan and bring to the boil. Reduce by half, then add the stock and reduce this by half again. Finally, add the brown sauce and finish by whisking in the butter.

Pour the reduced sauce around the toast to serve.

GRILLED KIPPERS WITH MUSTARD BUTTER

The Wolseley serves only the best kippers from the renowned Severn and Wye Smokery in Gloucestershire.

Serves 4

4 kippers
2 lemons, halved

For the mustard butter
75g Dijon mustard
75g wholegrain mustard
250g best-quality unsalted butter, at room temperature

First, make the mustard butter: mix the mustards into the butter and ensure that they are thoroughly combined. Roll in a piece of kitchen foil to make a cigar shape. Bring the ends together and twist, just like a sweet wrapper. Chill briefly in the freezer to firm up.

Preheat the grill to just above medium. Grill the kippers for 5–10 minutes, or until lightly coloured.

Put each kipper on a plate and top with 2 thick slices of the mustard butter. Serve with a lemon half.

Smoked Haddock Fishcakes
with Poached Eggs

Serves 4–6

250g undyed smoked haddock
250ml milk
1 onion
3 bay leaves
2 cloves
125g smoked salmon, cut into strips
125g waxy potatoes (The Wolseley uses La Ratte), cooked and peeled
125ml mayonnaise
25g capers
15g finely chopped dill
3 egg yolks
75g shallot, finely chopped
200g panko (Japanese coarse dried) breadcrumbs
juice of 1 lemon
vegetable oil, for frying
4–6 eggs
good dash of white-wine vinegar
20g chopped chives

Poach the haddock in the gently simmering milk with the onion, bay leaves and cloves until it flakes readily: about 5 minutes. Remove the haddock, flake the fish into a large mixing bowl and leave to cool.

Add all the remaining ingredients except the oil, whole eggs, vinegar and chives, reserving half of the breadcrumbs. Leave the mixture to rest for at least half an hour.

Form the mixture into 75g cakes, then roll these in the remaining breadcrumbs. Heat some vegetable oil in a large frying pan and fry the fishcakes until well-coloured on both sides and cooked through (you may need to do this in batches, or use 2 pans).

Poach the eggs using the vinegar as described on page 57. Serve the fishcakes with a poached egg on top and scattered with the chopped chives.

Lambs Kidneys with Madeira

Serves 4

8 lambs kidneys
milk, to cover
2 tablespoons flour, plus more for dusting
50g butter
2 large shallots, finely chopped
200ml hot chicken stock
salt and black pepper to taste
2 tablespoons Madeira
2 tablespoons double cream (optional)
triangles of toast, to serve
chopped parsley, to garnish

Soak the kidneys for an hour or two in just enough milk to cover. Drain and pare off the outer membrane, then cut each in half and remove the cores.

Season some flour with salt and pepper and dust the kidney halves in this, shaking off any excess.

Melt the butter in a large, heavy frying pan and sauté the kidneys until sealed on all sides. Transfer to a hot dish using a slotted spoon.

Add the chopped shallots to the butter in the pan and sauté until golden brown. Add the 2 tablespoons of flour, and then slowly pour in the hot stock. Season with salt and pepper, return the kidneys to the pan with the Madeira and simmer for 2–3 minutes.

Finish by stirring in the cream, if you are using it, and serve on toast triangles, sprinkled with chopped parsley.

CRÊPE COMPLET

Serves 4

For the crêpes
65g buckwheat flour
250g soft white flour (The Wolseley uses Moulbie T55 Blanche)
375ml homogenized milk
1 small egg

For the filling
4 large eggs
8 slices of cooked Ayrshire bacon
100g grated Gruyère cheese

Combine the crêpe ingredients by gently folding the liquid into the sieved dry ingredients, and loosen with a little water to produce a pouring consistency.

Rub the inside of a crêpe pan with a wad of kitchen paper moistened with sunflower oil. Place it over a moderate to high heat until good and hot, then pour a good ladleful of the batter into it. Tilt the pan to spread the batter out over the base. When you see the mixture firming and holes appearing in the crêpe, remove from the heat. Keep the crêpes warm in a low oven while you make 3 more.

Return the crêpes, one by one, to the pan. Crack an egg into the middle of each and arrange the cooked bacon around it, like a fence. Spread the cheese over the cooked egg and fold in the edges of the crêpe to form a parcel. Cook for 3–4 minutes longer.

Serve immediately.

WAFFLES WITH CARAMELISED BANANA

At The Wolseley, waffles are served this way or just with maple syrup or with added strips of grilled bacon. You can make chocolate waffles by adding melted chocolate to the butter, and cheese waffles by adding grated cheese. Vanilla and cinnamon are also often used to flavour waffle batter. You will, of course, need a waffle iron.

Makes about 8

275g plain flour
large pinch of salt
1 tablespoon sugar
4 teaspoons baking powder
2 large eggs, beaten
85g melted unsalted butter
275ml water
1 banana per serving
icing sugar, to dust and serve
maple syrup or crème fraîche, to serve

Sift the flour, salt, sugar and baking powder into a large mixing bowl. Make a well in the mixture, add the eggs and gradually incorporate them into the flour, adding the melted butter as you go. Add just enough of the water to achieve a smooth but firm batter the consistency of thick cream.

Preheat a waffle iron and spray it with cooking oil or melted butter (low-fat spray will do the job). Add a good ladleful of batter – it should just fill the iron. Have a tray underneath to collect any overspill.

The waffles cook in about 10 minutes. Keep hot in a low oven while you make the rest. Dust with icing sugar just before serving.

To prepare the banana, preheat a hot grill. Peel the banana, slice it in half lengthwise and place on a roasting tray. Coat liberally with icing sugar and grill until nicely coloured.

Place the caramelised banana on top of your waffles and dust with more icing sugar. If you like, you can finish with some maple syrup or crème fraîche.

FRUIT AND CEREALS

Directly above the Thermopylae of the kitchen pass, another one is duplicated in the dining room. This is where the lifts are sent. Here an assertive and energetic Egyptian holds his end of the pass. He shouts into the tinny intercom. Up here are all the makings of all the breakfast dishes that don't involve cooking: the fruit salads and cereals, mueslis, toasts, juices and the coffee machine. When you get your cappuccino it will more than likely have a pattern on it that looks like a foamy engraving of a New Zealand fern. This is both pretty and incongruous; it is the result of the small undulations of frothed milk as they're shuddered into the cup. There is a strip of chocolate powder: a very un-Italian adulteration.

If anything epitomizes the modern age's contribution and attitude to the breakfast table, then cereals do. They were invented in America. They are the result of converging changes in economy, society and technology. The puffing, cracking, extruding, shaping, colouring and sugaring of wheat and rice by cheap industrial processes came to feed a workforce that was itself being extruded, puffed, cracked and expanded by industrialization. Instant cereal suited a new world in a hurry. Healthy, clean, effortless, modern: an alternative to the variations of porridge and grits that had started the day for immigrant America. A breakfast of dehydrated cereal with the addition of a healthful cupful of pasturized milk wasn't just convenient, it was also practical, and a vote for the new – a belief in the future.

The cereal bowl invented a new stereotype for a meal: the morning rush, the fond image of a family in too much of a hurry to sit down and eat together, running through the kitchen grabbing boxes and bowls, all helter-skeltering to get on with the promise of ambition. They had new buses and new trains to catch, new offices and new schools to attend to become that new invention of the new age: commuters. Cereal was a signifier of a compact, efficient, time-strapped life, a dish that freed the consumer from the heavy manners of conversation over a table. It could be eaten standing up. You could eat it on your own. You could eat cereal without etiquette. You could eat it out of plastic with stainless steel. Cereal said a lot about you and your place in the New World.

It also answered the pressing fear of the new age: old age. Mr Kellogg came upon corn flakes because he was obsessed with health and his digestion: most precisely, his colonic health. The turn of the twentieth century saw – along with a marked improvement in plumbing, public health and potable water – a growing concern for bowel performance. Breakfast cereals were one of the first foods to be invented as being primarily good for you: medicinal first, enjoyable second. And they were specifically made for commercial production, not as adaptations of homemade. No one has ever tried to home-bake rice crispies, shred their own wheat, or cut out their own Cheerios. Kellogg launched his toasted cornflakes company in 1906, the same year that Coca-Cola replaced the cocaine in its drink with caffeine. There was the first radio broadcast in America – music, a poem and a talk – which could be heard only by ships' wireless operators. Ibsen died and Samuel Beckett was born. Paul Cézanne painted *The Gardener Vallier*, there was a great earthquake in San Francisco, and the word 'allergy' was coined by the Austrian paediatrician Clemens von Parquet, whose name still brings some people out in a rash.

Cereal grew to be an edible symbol of the life we live now, so that some day, if we got to work early enough and did well enough, we'd be able to afford a life where we could have porridge and kippers and eggs and bacon, and a second cappuccino and read the papers.

Cereal wasn't the first fast food, but it was the first food specifically designed to be eaten fast: a box that assumed you were late. It implied that food was not the prime priority of your life, but simply the fuel to make that life run efficiently.

Which is all very well, but 1906 marks a tectonic shift in the purpose and focus of food. Breakfast cereal cleverly invented a new demi-meal by promotion and advertising. Using that newfangled wireless when the ships' radio operators got bored with it, they convinced modern mothers that children needed a distinct and separate breakfast from grown-ups. Up until then, children had been weaned on small portions of adult food, but with cereal, there was a whole library of new boxes specifically for them, manufactured for their peculiar medical needs – which weren't their bowels. (Whoever wanted a child to have more efficient bowels?) Children's cereals had added vitamins and minerals – see how those two words roll off the tongue together? Vitamins were only just being discovered in time for breakfast.

On the dining-room display counter there is also a variety of mueslis and granolas, which always seem to be an Old World version of the New World original. Bircher muesli is just the edited highlights of cereals made unpleasantly wet and clammy. Personally, I find it difficult to eat cereal in a restaurant; somehow it's too intimate – too personal. You should eat cereal staring sightlessly out of the window with your dressing gown hanging open.

Then there is yoghurt, a substance that Evelyn Waugh once memorably and definitively noticed 'tasted so foul it simply had to be good for you'. Yoghurt is an ingredient that has transubstantiated from being the sour mother-in-law of cheese to being an entire clinic in a tub. Yoghurt from 'off' goats milk, they say, can specifically reduce cholesterol. Yoghurt can cure heartburn, make you thinner, put a *cordon sanitaire* around farts and, if applied externally, alleviate thrush and give a nice antiquated and distressed patina to shiny bronze. Yoghurt is the elixir of vitality and prolonged youth for humans, but premature ageing for coal scuttles.

PRUNE AND ELDERFLOWER COMPOTE

Compotes are dishes of fresh or dried fruit that have been briefly cooked (or, as here, steeped) in a light syrup. Unlike 'stewed fruit', the fruits in compotes are normally left whole or in large chunks. Interestingly, early British cookbooks refer to them as 'composts' – both words come from the same French word for 'bringing together' – but, as the word compost became increasingly used by gardeners (with all the related connotations). Use of 'compote' began to replace the earlier, earthier term in culinary circles.

Serves 4

> *350g prunes*
> *50g caster sugar*
> *100ml water*
> *5 tablespoons elderflower cordial*
> *yoghurt, to serve*

Soak the prunes in hot water for about 20 minutes.

Meanwhile make a light sugar syrup by mixing the sugar with the water in a small pan and heating gently until all the sugar is dissolved.

Drain the water from the prunes, then add the elderflower cordial and the syrup and mix well.

Serve with yoghurt.

BIRCHER MUESLI

Serves about 4 *(you can easily scale quantities up or down)*

> *125g dried muesli mix (you can use a proprietary brand or simply use*
> *   rolled oats or a mix of oats and other grains, like wheat or rye flakes)*
> *30g (about 2 tablespoons) runny honey*
> *30g unsweetened dried cranberries or dried cherries*
> *25g sultanas*
> *25g ground hazelnuts*
> *250ml milk*
> *125ml double cream*
> *1 apple, grated*
> *1 pear, grated*

Combine all the ingredients thoroughly in a large bowl.

Refrigerate for 1–2 hours, or preferably overnight, to allow the muesli to absorb the liquids. If it is quite dry in the morning, as most of the liquids have been absorbed, you can add a little more milk if you like.

Serve with more honey or some maple syrup, seasonal berries, sliced dried or fresh figs and/or yoghurt.

Note
If you need to make only enough for one or two people, then mix only the muesli, dried fruit and nuts. Then, each evening you can make up a batch of that for the next morning by stirring in some honey, milk, cream and fresh fruit. However, it does keep well for several days even after the liquids have been added. After two days, though, so much of the liquids will have been absorbed that you may have to add more milk.

Variations
You can use all sorts of dried fruit in muesli: raisins or prunes, dried apples, apricots, bananas, dates, pears, mango or pineapple. Chopped or grated Brazil nuts, coconut, pecans or walnuts, and seeds such as sesame and sunflower also make good additions.

GRANOLA

Granola is basically a type of cooked muesli and, like muesli, it can vary widely in its actual mix of constituents. Generally, however, it is more highly sweetened to give a crunchy coating to its grains, nuts and seeds. The Wolseley serves a fairly classic mix based on rolled oats and flavoured with orange zest and vanilla.

Serves 2

30g demerara sugar
20g (about 1 tablespoon) honey
10g (about 2 teaspoons) golden syrup
20g butter
40g rolled oats
30g desiccated coconut
25g pecans
15g flaked almonds
10g pistachio nuts
10g chopped hazelnuts
10g sunflower seeds
grated zest of ½ orange
½ teaspoon vanilla essence
yoghurt and/or fresh berries, to serve

Preheat the oven to 150°C or gas mark 2.

In a deep baking tray, mix the sugar, honey, syrup and butter, and put in the oven for 1 minute.

Remove the tray from the oven and mix in the remaining ingredients.

Bake for 35–40 minutes until golden, turning the mixture every 5 minutes.

Serve with yoghurt and fresh berries.

PORRIDGE

Serves 4

1 cup of oats (if using rolled or 'instant' oats, follow packet instructions
*   as to cooking time)*
3½– 4 cups (depending on how thick you like it) water or milk, or a mixture
1 teaspoon salt
more salt and milk or cream, to serve

As with rice, it is easier and usually gives better results to use volume measures
for both the oats and the cooking liquid. Some people soak the oatmeal overnight
in plenty of cold water.

You can sprinkle the oats into the simmering liquid, but it seems to produce much
the same results if you just mix the oats and liquid in a pan over a moderate heat
until simmering, and then continue to simmer, stirring regularly, for 10 minutes.

At this point add the salt (even if you are going to serve the porridge sweet).
Add this any earlier and you risk hardening the exterior of the oats so that they
won't absorb liquid as easily to become creamy. Continue to simmer for about
5–10 minutes more – again, depending on how thick you like it.

Pour into serving bowls and let stand for a minute or two. Serve with more salt
(or sugar) and milk or cream, or any of the other additions mentioned below.

Variations
Adding some fresh, dried or cooked fruit – such as bananas, berries, raisins or
sultanas, puréed cooked apples or chopped dried apricots – does make sweetened
porridge an even more nutritious way to start the day. You can also use fruit juice
as the cooking liquid: orange, for example, if adding berries, or apple if mixing in
dried fruit.

TEA, COFFEE AND HOT CHOCOLATE

Along with the thirteen varieties of coffee you could order for breakfast at The Wolseley, not to mention the nine teas, four infusions and three milk shakes, there are also five versions of hot chocolate. The grandest is picked out in red on the menu to indicate a particularly splendid confection. This is chocolate gourmand. It comes as frothy hot milk in a jug and a thick, intense ganache of chocolate in another jug which you mix together, like Dr Jekyll, in a glass with a little whisk.

Chocolate has rather fallen out of fashion as a breakfast drink. The Spanish still gamely chug a particularly thick version with long doughnuts. In the eighteenth century, though, in London, chocolate would have been the breakfast drink of choice for the leisured classes. It has moved to become the late-night drink for children. No ingredient has made such an extreme journey, both physically and metaphorically, as chocolate.

It was originally drunk by the Aztecs as a votive communion, spiked with chilli and butter and served hot, rather like the *mole* sauce that Mexicans still cook with. Only men were allowed to taste it. The Spanish took cocoa back to Europe. *En route* it crossed the paths of ships taking a plant from North Africa the other way, one that had been long cultivated by the Arabs. Its crystallized juice had a huge value in Europe, but there was a limited supply. It was a preservative for delicate fruits through the long winters: sugar. And sugar would transform the economy of the Caribbean. (That and two other imports, measles and influenza, which wiped out the Arawaks and what was left of the Caribs...)

So a new workforce was needed to harvest the sugar, and it was imported as slaves from Africa. The sugar was mixed with the cocoa and made chocolate: the most successful manufactured food in the history of the world, the most desired and the most resisted. Nothing else had been transformed into so many separate dishes. There are more cookbooks devoted to chocolate than to every other crop combined.

The Spanish tried to keep its manufacture secret, but soon it was out all over Europe and became one of the first great food fads. The world's largest exporter of cocoa is now not South America but West Africa (Ghana and the Ivory Coast) whence came the original slaves for the New World.

The Viennese-style chocolate at the Wolseley is about as close as you'll ever get to the stuff that was drunk in the chocolate houses in Piccadilly and St James's 200 years ago. You can ask to have it with a tot of rum: another drink that was invented by the cultivation of sugar.

Sugar prices fluctuated wildly throughout the seventeenth and eighteenth centuries, making spectacular new millionaires and equally spectacular bankruptcies. Rum was invented to create a market for surplus sugar. Originally, it was sold to passing ships, whose crews added it to their sour fresh water to make it palatable, and it became known as *grog*, named after the grogram overcoat worn by Admiral Edward Vernon, who substituted the watered rum for the neat stuff in the British naval ration.

It was issued twice a day: a quarter-pint of rum to a pint of water. Half a pint of rum a day is a pretty good party, and it was cut in 1824 to once a day, then to half a gill in 1850, and stopped for officers (who, presumably, had their own supplies) altogether in 1881. For warrant officers it came to an end in 1918. The grog ration finally was abandoned by the Navy altogether in 1970, cutting a tie to the West Indies that went back to Walter Raleigh and the Black Triangle of the slave trade. It had been the Dutch courage for fighting the horrifying, wind-driven, black-powder, iron-and-wood naval engagements.

Grogram is an Anglicization of the French *gros grain*, or coarse grain: a cloth mixed from silk and mohair stiffened with gum, invariably made in black. It's not worn much by admirals now, but is still used in ladies' couture. And rum and chocolate are still two flavours that cleave to each other with long, bittersweet memories.

COFFEE TYPES AND TERMINOLOGY

~ **Affogato**, meaning 'drowned', is espresso served over ice cream.

~ **Americano** is espresso topped with hot water to the strength of filter coffee.

~ **Café crème** is an espresso with added steamed milk served in a coffee cup.

~ **Cappuccino** is the much-loved Italian frothy coffee, an espresso shot of coffee topped with perfectly foamed hot milk and foam.

~ **Con panna** is coffee topped with whipped cream.

~ **Corretto**, meaning 'corrected', is espresso with added alcohol, usually grappa, brandy or sambuca.

~ **Crema** is the nut-brown foamy layer on top of a well-made espresso.

~ **Doppio**, meaning 'double', is two shots of espresso in one cup.

~ **Einspänner** is a *lungo* (see below) topped with whipped cream.

~ **Espresso** is a strong, short coffee, approx. 45 ml; the delicate flavour of the coffee is extracted through high pressure.

~ **Latte**, meaning 'milk', can be made two ways: an espresso topped with hot milk and a drizzle of foam or a hot glass of milk with an espresso shot poured in to make a 3-layered look.

~ **Lungo**, meaning 'long', is an espresso made with more than the usual amount of water (about double) passing through the ground coffee, producing a weaker drink.

~ **Macchiato** meaning 'marked' or 'stained', is an espresso with a teaspoon of milk and foam on top.

~ **Marocchino** is an espresso topped with hot milk and foam, covered in cocoa powder, best served in a glass.

~ **Mocha** is a rich hot chocolate, topped with an espresso, hot milk and foam.

~ **Ristretto**, meaning 'shortened', is an espresso made with less water, yielding a coffee that has more essential oils and flavour with less caffeine and potential bitterness, a more full-bodied potent taste.

THE PERFECT CUP OF COFFEE

~ Whenever possible, buy whole beans and only grind them as and when required. For the necessary freshness, buy from a speciality coffee roaster/retailer in your local area, or alternatively in vaccuum packed bags (and you can now buy good coffee online).

~ Always store coffee at room temperature, away from light, heat and cold, in an airtight container.

~ Clean all equipment thoroughly between each use.

~ The water should not be at boiling point when it hits the coffee grounds, but just off the boil.

~ The longer the water is going to be in contact with the coffee, the coarser the grind should be. Therefore, a cafetière requires a coarse grind, as the coffee is immersed in the water for up to 5 minutes before the cafetière is plunged. Filter coffee requires a finer grind because the water passes through the filters at a faster rate. Espresso coffee machines need the finest of grinds because the extraction process is about 25 seconds.

~ Be sure to regularly sharpen your grinder's blades as bluntness will result in burnt flavours.

~ Warm espresso cups beforehand with a splash of very hot water.

~ Don't keep brewed coffee over even the gentlest of heats for more than 20 minutes or it will become bitter. A Thermos flask or an insulated coffee pot will help.

~ Always use white granulated sugar. Brown sugar affects the taste too much.

Arabica versus Robusta

Arabica and Robusta are the two basic coffee varieties. Arabica beans are generally grown high in the mountains and their cultivation requires a great deal of care, so they are necessarily more expensive than Robusta, which is comparatively easy to grow and isn't restricted to high altitudes.

Arabica is undoubtedly the coffee with the more complex flavour, while Robusta, as its name suggests, is a simple, strong, 'one-note' coffee. Robusta dominates most inexpensive blends and instant coffees, so its slightly bitter taste is what the majority of the population think of as 'coffee'.

Premium coffee blends are very high in Arabica, but do also usually need a kick of Robusta to bring the drink to life.

TEA TYPES AND TERMINOLOGY

~ **White tea** is a rare type of tea produced on a limited scale in China and Sri Lanka, unfermented and as close to its natural state from picking, it is high in antioxidants. Its name derives from its silvery colour.

~ **Green tea** is derived from leaves that are dried fresh from picking. In this state, much of tea's health-giving antioxidant content is preserved. The refreshing taste of green teas is best enjoyed without any additions. Brew them in water that has come off the boil and infuse for 3–4 minutes.

~ **Oolong** is a sort of halfway house between green and black teas, large-leaved teas that are allowed to ferment slightly.

~ **Black tea** is made by wilting the leaves, then bruising them so they ferment fully and oxidize (like a fruit turning brown) before drying. Apart from lapsang souchong and Darjeeling, most black teas are strong enough to cope with added milk or lemon.

~ **The Wolseley's English Breakfast Blend** is a blend of Assam and Ceylon black teas. The rich strength of the Assam and the smooth briskness of the Ceylon combine to produce a fully rounded flavour.

~ **The Wolseley Afternoon Blend** is a fine balance of China black tea with the subtle honey and chestnut of Formosa Oolong and the delicacy of Darjeeling to make a rich, flavoursome cup with a delicate and refined elegance.

~ **Assam tea** from the flood plains of the Brahmaputra River in this northeast Indian province is rich and full-bodied, often said to possess a distinct maltiness. It is favoured by those who like to drink tea with or after their meals.

~ **Ceylon tea** from Sri Lanka is light and refreshing, with a delicate crisp, citrussy flavour. It makes perfect afternoon tea.

~ **Darjeeling tea**, grown on the foothills of the Himalayas, is often termed the champagne of teas – it has a rich gentle flavour for a black tea, with a delicate flowery aroma. It is best enjoyed without milk or lemon.

~ **Earl Grey** is a blend of predominantly China black tea scented with oil of bergamot to yield a very refreshing, flowery, citrussy tea, suitable for the afternoon. Aficionados have it without milk or lemon, but it can be taken with either.

~ **Lapsang souchong** is a strong black tea, speciality of China's Fujian province. The fermented leaves are smoked over slow-smouldering pine wood – a rich and pungent smokey tea with robust body.

~ **Jasmine tea** is made by infusing green or oolong teas with jasmine blossom flowers. The refreshing, flowery, citrussy flavour makes it an ideal palate cleanser.

THE PERFECT CUP OF TEA

~ Always use loose leaves. Loose leaf teas impart the true flavour of a tea and infuse and brew better.

~ Always use fresh cold water brought to the boil, this maintains the water's oxygen levels and is essential for proper brewing. (If your water is particularly hard, it is best to use a filter or filtered water.)

~ Pre-heat the pot just before the water comes to the boil, pour a little water into the pot to heat it and then tip the water out, replacing the lid.

~ Use the correct measurements and ratio of water to tea: 1 teaspoon of tea leaves per person and 1 for the pot. Water should normally reach the internal base of the teapot spout as a guideline. Be aware that broken leaves as opposed to whole leaves will impart a stronger flavour so a little more water is advisable if using them.

~ Pour at the boil. With black teas it is essential to pour as soon as the kettle reaches the boil, replacing the lid on the tea-pot to avoid any heat loss. (For green and white teas water should be off the boil.)

~ Know your brewing times. Once made the tea should be allowed to infuse for the correct time before drinking - tea served too quickly will dilute the taste, tea brewed too long will add bitterness. A general rule is black teas 3–5 minutes, white 7–15 minutes, green 3–4 minutes.

~ Milk, sugar, lemon. Some teas, such as strong black teas from India and Sri Lanka, can be enhanced by adding milk. Some green teas, such as Gunpowder, can have honey or mint added; others, including white and scented teas, are best served in their natural state, with no additions.

Milk: before or after…?

Milk in before or after pouring tea? There is no doubt that the two practices give very different taste results. The fats in milk are affected in different ways by either having very hot tea poured slowly into the milk, so that these fats never overheat, or by suddenly plunging milk into a large cup of hot tea. Some also claim that adding the milk afterwards alters the milk proteins, yielding a slightly stale taste. Proponents of adding milk afterwards counter that putting the milk in first gives a milkier, more caramelized flavour that dominates the taste of the tea. Perhaps the most decisive argument is that it is much easier to judge the correct quantity of milk in relation to the strength of the brew when adding afterwards. The Wolseley favours this approach.

HOT CHOCOLATE

Serves 1

For 1 x 300ml glass
  10ml cold milk
  10ml whipping cream
  30g good-quality chocolate (but not too bitter)
  220ml hot milk with foam

Bring the cold milk and the cream to the boil in a small saucepan.

Place the chocolate in another saucepan or heatproof bowl. Pour the milk and cream mixture on top and mix well.

Add the hot milk with foam, such as that which has been frothed up with a coffee machine or a whisk.

Stir gently to mix and serve with two chocolate sticks on the side, if you like.

CHOCOLATE FONDANT

This little bombshell of intense chocolate flavour is the perfect way to get that morning kick if you can't drink coffee – or if you just happen to prefer chocolate. It is best served in an espresso cup, as it is more or less its chocolate equivalent, and no more than that quantity is required. The sweetened thick, dark drinking chocolate powder needed is normally made by Italian and Spanish manufacturers, and you are more likely to find it in good coffee and chocolate shops.

Serves 1

1 heaped teaspoon good-quality thick, dark drinking-chocolate powder
2 teaspoons double cream
4 teaspoons hot water

Blend all the ingredients in a small bowl set over simmering water until uniformly hot and the mixture develops a thick, custard-like consistency.

Spoon into a warmed espresso cup to serve, and sup with a teaspoon.

As the clock moves towards seven o'clock and opening, the staff check their stations for the last time. The muesli and the sugar, the honey-pourers that look like children's rattles, the antique silver tea- and coffee-pots, the strainers that revolve in their own saucers, the little *confiture* pots of raspberry jam, chocolate spread, lemon curd and marmalade, the yoghurt bowls, the fresh fruit salad, the compote of prunes, the menus, the napery.

It's seven. The doors are opened, and thirty seconds later the first customer walks in. Pinstriped and briefcased, already furrowed of brow, he barely looks at the waiter, who, knowing him as a regular, walks to a familiar table. He unfolds the *Financial Times,* orders tea and cereal. The day has begun.

The first people in will be sober-suited businessmen who do focused, brief meetings with each other. They don't linger. Their business is business and they need to get on. By 8.30 the businesspeople will be in the people business. The suits get slightly trendier, the room grows less masculine, the noise level goes up, but oddly, it also becomes more conspiratorial. There are a lot of tables here for people who couldn't meet in their offices. There are tentative job interviews, business gossip, competitors sounding each other out. There is the odd table of furtive couples who left the office together and who arrived back here together, still wearing yesterday's clothes. They snigger and stare into each other's eyes before pretending they came on different buses. There are a few agents poaching authors, media people pitching TV programmes and journalists listening off-the-record.

By ten, most of those who have offices to go to have gone and the meetings become PR-related. There are more women than men. And then there are the out-of-town ladies come for sales or galleries, mothers and daughters looking for bridesmaids' dresses, families of Germans with cultural lists, pairs of Italians in search of cashmere. Now breakfast becomes more voluptuous, more of a special occasion: they're ordering Champagne and orange and cakes.

By twelve, breakfast is over. The lovingly crafted *Viennoiserie* is cleared away and taken down to the staff dining room. The waiters start laying up for lunch.

Breakfast doesn't stop all at once; it recedes like a tide.

Publishing Director Jane O'Shea
Creative Director Helen Lewis
Designer Claire Peters
Photographer David Loftus
Design Consultant Pete King
Project Editor Jamie Ambrose
Production Marina Asenjo

Published in 2008 by Quadrille, an imprint of Hardie Grant Publishing

First published in 2008 by
Quadrille
52–54 Southwark Street
London SE1 1UN
quadrille.com

Reprinted in 2009, 2010, 2011, 2013, 2014 (twice), 2015, 2016, 2017,
2018, 2019
19 18 17 16 15 14 13 12

Cataloguing in Publication Data: a catalogue record for this book is
available from the British Library.

ISBN 978 1 84400 444 7

Printed in China